FROM THE
COMPASS
TO THE CROSS

The story of secret societies, conspiracy theories
and fraternal organisations

DENIS CALDERWOOD

FROM THE
COMPASS
TO THE CROSS

The story of secret societies, conspiracy theories
and fraternal organisations

G2 rights ltd

G2 rights ltd

From the compass to the cross
Copyright ©Denis Calderwood 2012

First edition published in the UK in September 2012
© G2 Rights Limited 2012
www.G2rights.co.uk

Print Edition ISBN: 978-1-78281-006-3

G2 Rights Ltd, Unit 9 Whiffens Farm, Clement Street, Hextable, Kent, BR8 7PG

FROM THE
COMPASS
TO THE
CROSS

CONTENTS

INTRODUCTION

When people look at secret societies they see conspiracy as a way of explaining how the world operates, with certain groups manipulating the levers of power. In this book I seek to debunk such theories.

I have examined the interconnections between secret societies and fraternities. I had a particular interest in the Knights of St John of Jerusalem (sometimes called the Knights of Malta), and this led me to explore their origin. This research encompassed the Orders known as the Royal Black Institution of Ireland, the Loyal Orange Institution, the Royal Arch Purple Order and the Ancient Order of Free and Accepted Masons.

During this process I have referred to the political and religious conditions which formed the background to their emergence. Specifically, I examined Ireland, Scotland and England from the 17th century onwards. The significance of the tradition of dissent in Ireland and Scotland and the rise of the United Irishmen are central to some aspects of this development.

The Irish and Scottish diaspora to the New World of North America, when members of these organisations emigrated and set up branches of the Orders, are an important element in this story.

The book will attempt to place the rituals and ceremonies of the Orders in a Biblical context which will explain the significance of a movement in thought and belief from the Judaic culture of the Old Testament to that of a Christian New Testament.

The centrality of these two books and the changes in meaning of the term TEMPLE are key elements in the question as to why the rituals and ceremonies of a Christian Order of Knighthood refer to the notion of a 'physical' Temple as well as a 'spiritual' Temple, an important element in the movement of thought and understanding between the Patriarchal Era and the Christian Era.

CHAPTER ONE

SECRET SOCIETIES, CONSPIRACY THEORY AND FRATERNAL SOCIETIES

Today there are many people who believe that secret societies are operating across the world in the areas of politics, finance and education. This is not a new phenomenon; it can be found in the history of many countries and nations. Linked to these thoughts is a belief that unpleasant events can be attributed to such organisations.

It is my contention that there are people who seek an explanation for changes or events in society by claiming that they are the result of the workings of a secret society or societies. I assert that this is largely a consequence of the fact that historians and other commentators, from the 20th century onwards, have tended to ignore explanations regarding secret societies and influence as paranoid-driven explanations, unworthy of serious analysis. Such an approach has led to the unintended consequence of an open season for conspiracy theorists.

Although the term conspiracy literally means 'to act or think in harmony', in more recent times it has come to have a more sinister connotation, ie to plan together in secret, possibly with the aim of committing an illegal or evil action.

This development has been fuelled by recent disclosures such as events in the political reign of former US President John Kennedy. In their book *Ultimate Sacrifices*, Lamor Wadron and Thom Hartmann claim that in the spring of 1963, John and Robert Kennedy started laying the foundations for a coup against Fidel Castro, the Cuban leader, codenamed 'AMWORLD'. They claim that Robert was in charge of the operation and that the American Department of Defence was to be responsible for its implementation. This operation would involve the use of Mafia 'hitmen' to assassinate Castro and replace him with a provisional government. However, the Mafia were angry with the Kennedys, because Robert was pursuing them and Jack had been the target of two attempts on his life.

Another consequence has been that certain religious and ethnic groups have become a target for oppression and misrepresentation. Leaving aside the whole nonsense of racial purity or impurity, this has not stopped attempts to oppress or misrepresent such groups, for example the publication *of The Protocols of the Elders of Zion*, a forgery created by Yuliana Glinka in Paris before 1895. This document claimed to be a secret plan by a council of rabbis intent on taking over the world. It was embraced by many adherents of anti-semitism in the early part of the last century. However, in his book *Jewish Thought: An Introduction*, Professor Oliver Leaman suggests that although *The Protocols of the Elders of Zion* is factually inaccurate, in the modern world the Jews are few in number yet very successful and able to exercise influence, particularly on the political scene. Thus his statement that 'a small group of Jews can manipulate gentiles to do their bidding is not wholly invalid'.

A cursory glance at the world of high finance with its

Rothschilds, Warburgs and Lazards and the decisive role played by George Soros in speculation on the fiscal markets add fuel to such views in the eyes of some people. Other so-called 'secret forces' have included the Society of Jesus, the Freemasons, the CIA, Opus Dei, the Roman Catholic Knights of Malta (whose membership has included former directors of the Central Intelligence Agency William Casey and John McCone and the former US Secretary of State Alexander Haig - see *Rule by Secrecy*, Jim Marrs, p.256 ff for a fuller discussion).

Within the Roman Catholic Church the role of Opus Dei, the 'Work of God', is viewed in some quarters with suspicion. Opus Dei is a secret organisation founded by Josemaria de Escriva de Balanguer in Franco's Spain, and supports conservatism. Cardinal Wojtyla, later Pope John Paul II, gave it the status of an independent world diocese, and later canonised its founder. The present Pope, when he was Cardinal Ratzinger, was given a honorary doctorate from the Spanish Opus Dei University.

Conspiracy also surrounds the role played by the secret Masonic lodge P 2 and the strange circumstances surrounding the death of one of its members, Roberto Calvi, nicknamed 'God's Banker', the head of Italy's largest private bank, when it went bankrupt (see Hans Kung Chapter X for a fuller discussion). Another writer, David Yallop, in his book *In God's Name*, reflects on the Vatican's entanglement in the world of finance and the Mafia. The sudden death of Pope John Paul I at the age of 67 when in office for only 33 days, which was not investigated by the police or subject to an autopsy, helps to feed conspiracy theorists' speculations.

Today, perhaps the most popular targets for such theorists are the Knights Templar and their so-called descendants. Hence the popularity of the themes of the novels of Dan Browne and others.

So what are the characteristics of a secret society? Firstly, it is of course secret. Generally speaking one cannot access its written records in order to examine its work and influence. Secondly, it is only open to those who have been initiated in some way or other. Thirdly, if one could have access to the working of such societies it is possible that unfamiliarity with the context would make it difficult, if not impossible, to understand its relevance. By their very nature the rituals and symbolic structures are only relevant to those initiated into the 'mysteries' in a specific context. This is not unlike the argument that the Roman Catholic Mass is only fully understood by its communicants, as are other such rituals in various religions.

In the light of such features, perhaps it would be sensible to cease to use the term 'secret society' and in its place refer to societies with secrets. The secrets are those elements which are fully understood only by those who take part in the process or rituals. Such an explanation may enable one to move away from the notion of conspiracy and instead allow an examination of the rituals and symbolism as less threatening phenomena which can perhaps be placed in a historical, social and cultural context.

The concept of societies with rituals which have a secret meaning are as old as mankind. Perhaps the oldest are the cave paintings of Lascaux (France) and Altamira (Spain) which have puzzled scholars since they were discovered. Successive generations have pondered over whether the images refer to actions, events or are symbolic of communication only understood by those holding special knowledge. According to some anthropologists, they are depictions of cosmological significance which reflect the manner in which palaeolithic people viewed their world.

In reality, in many primitive societies, it was a shaman (a person who was thought to be able to communicate with the spirit world) who interpreted the meanings of symbolic patterns, as it was he who was deemed to have these specific powers. In more recent historical times, shamanism was the indigenous religion of the people, for example, from Lapland to the Bering Straits. It was also used to denote the religious practices of North American Indians and the native populations of Australia. A basic feature is a belief in a multiplicity of spirits (animism) and the after-death existence of souls. A shaman was a person who, through a process of initiation, had obtained an authority over certain spirits and dressed in an appropriately symbolic form.

In the modern world the list of societies with secret rituals includes the secular student societies of Yale University, such as Skull and Bones, founded in 1832 and originally called the Eulogian Club after its patron, Eulogia, goddess of eloquence. Its membership was restricted to male students until 1991, when the first female members were admitted. Its current members refer to each other as ' knights' and former members are termed 'patriarchs' (see Greer, p. 562 for a fuller discussion). The club has featured in such recent films as *The Good Shepherd* and *W*.

In the eyes of some conspiracy theorists, the Eulogian Club is America's most powerful secret organisation, largely because its members have included the two Bush presidents and because of its supposed links to the Council on Foreign Relations (CFR), a think tank. The latter was founded in 1921 and arose out of a series of meetings conducted during World War I. Its 'invitation only' membership is a representative sample of influential leaders in finance, communications and academia, and its journal, *Foreign Affairs*, is considered by many to be the most prestigious publication in its field. This organisation hosts regular luncheon meetings where prominent figures address its members on subjects of interest. For a fuller discussion I would refer the reader to Robbins A. (2002), *Secrets of the Tomb: Skull and Cross Bones, the Ivy League and the Hidden Paths of Power*.

Another organisation of similar structure and supposed sphere of influence is the Bilderberg Group, which was created in 1954 by Prince Bernhard of the Netherlands, holding its first meeting in the Bilderberg Hotel (see Greer, p. 106). Past chairmen have included Lord Peter Carrington, one time former UK Conservative Cabinet Minister, Secretary General of NATO and President of the Royal Institute of International Affairs (see Marrs p 41). According to Giles Radice, the British politician, Denis Healey was a founder member of the Bilderberg Conferences (p 85), which brought together North American and European leaders (pp 85-6).

In Edna Healey's book *Part of a Pattern* (p 262) she describes annual meetings organised by Menos and Pia Zombanakis in which 'informed and influential people from all parts of the world', including her husband Denis Healey, the former Labour Chancellor of the Exchequer, met to discuss the complex links of the financial world. Meetings of groups with this type of financial and political content are as manna from heaven to the conspiracy theorists. Such people like the gaps in our knowledge to be filled with wonder and speculation about 'hidden forces' with influence. If not secretly manipulating the world, they are perceived as having anti-democratic influences and features.

Guilds had emerged during the Middle Ages as associations of craftsmen specific to a trade, usually in a single town. There were three classes of membership; the masters, who had expert knowledge of their craft; the journeymen, fellows or companions, depending on the type of craft or trade, who had the basic skills and worked for a master for a daily wage; and finally the apprentices, who were learning the trade.

The guilds collected subscriptions from their members to provide welfare support to their families in the event of death. Each guild had its own symbols and legends relating to its origins. All three types of members had to undergo initiation rituals.

In France the guild structure, under the pressure of a rapidly changing society, broke down when the journeymen could no longer advance to master status. Thus emerged the Compagnonnage (from compagnon = companion, the standard French term for a journeyman). The first written traces of the compagnonnage are to be found in the twelfth century after the Council of Troyes. The document mentioned the most qualified workers as 'les Compagnons du Saint Devoir de Dieu'.

These brotherhoods of campagnonnage had their own initiation rituals, patron saints and elected officers. Within a brotherhood there were three associations; the Children of Père Soubise, the Children of Maître Jacques and the Children of Solomon. The members contributed to a fund for a welfare structure which helped companions during sickness and supported the families of deceased members. During the 17th and 18th centuries they were common throughout France, but in the 19th century they were largely replaced by the trade union movement. However, at the present time they are still widely dispersed across the main towns of France, with an office in Paris: La Federation Nationale Compagnonnique des Métiers du Bâtiment, 7 Rue Petit, 75019 Paris.

In Scotland the guilds were called incorporations and in

London, companies. During the 14th and 15th centuries in Scotland, tradesmen, craftsmen and artisans organised themselves into a trade, guild or incorporation, with their own charter, called a 'Seal of Cause'. The charter specified their rules and regulations and this in turn became their constitution.

Membership of these incorporations was restricted and attempts were made to look after and control their business interests. Out of this developed social care of the members, either if they were unemployed or to provide support to the families of deceased members. Each incorporation had its own banners and badges, or rituals, based on the tools of the trade. The use of rituals, ceremony and elements of secrecy served to differentiate members from the rest of society.

Not all groups of workers had this type of protection. In the earlier 16th century some followed the example of masons and with their lodges provided benefits by a levy fund or 'box fund' (these 'box' societies later became known as fraternities).

Historically it is very difficult to state with accuracy when they first appeared. It is possible that Friendly Societies originated in Scotland, probably in the 16th century. In 1555 there is evidence of the Incorporation of Carters, in Leith, enrolling journeymen. In England, it is very likely that these societies grew out of the mutual benefit societies of the Huguenots who had fled persecution in France in the 1680s. The Irish societies were more political in their nature and had much in common with religious divisions, whereas in Wales the link was more with language, for example, the Philanthropic Order of True Ivorites.

The 18th century witnessed the growth of Friendly Societies, which developed against a background of national industrial growth and imperial expansion. They helped to replace a reliance among certain sections of society upon the guilds and the system of alms giving. Through these societies the working and middle classes sought protection against deprivation. They were a form of insurance to provide sickness and death benefits. Deeply rooted in the concept of fellowship, ie the sharing of mutual interests and activities, the Friendly Societies met in public houses and developed public and private rituals. They soon laid down roots.

By 1800 these societies had became widespread and closely resembled the lodges of Freemasons in structure and codes of conduct. Some of these societies, such as the Oddfellows, claimed biblical origins, while the Order of Rechabites, a non-drinking friendly society, claimed its origins to be in ancient Egypt. In the same historical period the link between Friendly Societies and public houses was well established, hence today we still find names such as the Gardener's Arms.

With the spread of the temperance movement, Friendly Societies emerged which were not based in such establishments. In America the Independent Order of Good Templars became quite influential, and in England, the British Temperance Association. Women's friendly societies, although numerous in the 18th century, declined after 1800, largely as a consequence of male legal and political structures. A married woman could not legally own property and thus could not be guaranteed possession of the benefits.

A possible explanation as to why some of these societies claimed a connection with the past was that in the rapidly-changing economic and political climate of the times, a form of nostalgia for a more imagined past gave stability and meaning to life. A fuller discussion of such origins will be dealt with in later chapters when the rituals and symbolism of other organisations will be examined.

CHAPTER TWO

THE ORIGINS OF THE ORANGE ORDER

It is not the purpose of this study to deal with the events or the background of the conflict between William III and James II. I do, however, acknowledge that many of the these events are portrayed on the banners and huge Lambeg drums of Orange lodges and other organisations, such as the Royal Black Institution, as well as in paintings on the gable walls in cities, towns and villages in Northern Ireland. Although they are clearly an important aspect of the folk traditions and culture of Protestant Ireland, they are not central to this study. Nevertheless, in order to understand more fully why the Orange Order emerged, it is necessary to refer to the following developments.

After the victory of William III at the Battle of the Boyne in 1690 and the ending of the war a year later, the victors met to commemorate their success. By then they had formed themselves into informal clubs or societies. The overall term used to describe them was the Boyne Society.

In 1701 in Dublin, a statue was unveiled of William III in College Green, outside the Irish House of Parliament. According to J T Gilbert, the religious and political significance of the statue was reflected in the various medals and certificates of the Orange Association in 1795 (quoted on p 11 of *The History of the Royal Arch Purple Order*, henceforth referred to as HRAPO).

Ireland in the period 1750-1800, in particular the province of Ulster, had benefited from the peace that ensued after 1691. As a consequence of the success of the linen industry, the population increased and, generally speaking, living standards improved. By 1791 Belfast had a population of around 18,000 and a mainly Presbyterian middle class which was adding a radical dimension to the political climate of the times (J Bardon, A *History of Ulster*, p 203). These Ulster Presbyterians were, in the main, descendents of migrants from Lowland Scotland.

After the Reformation the inhabitants of this region had become either Calvinists or Presbyterians, with an emphasis on individual conscience and independence. Inevitably these beliefs tended to result in schism and with it the potential for religious, political and social conflict. Therefore it is perhaps true to say that the Anglicans of 18th century Ireland would have preferred to deal with Roman Catholics, with their view of society as a predetermined structure, rather than the concept of a democratically-elected oligarchy, as held by the Presbyterians.

In the rural parts of the province events were not always harmonious. In 1761 groups of farmers and weavers, the so called 'Hearts of Oak', rose in revolt against the 'cass', or local rate. This rate was used to make new roads and when it was increased the disquiet spread. The advance of industrial progress was also leading to social tensions, and when trade took a downturn in 1770 events reached a crisis point. Some farmers formed the 'Hearts of Steel' and the Irish Parliament was forced to use the military to crush the revolt. Many poorer people attempted to flee to America. By this time emigration to America had become an option; for example, between 1718-1775 the famine had forced thousands of Ulster Presbyterians across the Atlantic Ocean in search of a better life (see R J Dickson, *Ulster Emigration to Colonial America 1718-1775*).

Consequently, when the American Revolutionary War began in 1775 its ideals were treated with sympathy by the Ulster Presbyterian population. But in 1778, when France, the Roman Catholic arch-enemy of England, lent its support to the American rebels, such feelings of loyalty were severely questioned and challenged. It was against such a background and with the possibility of a French invasion on Irish shores that a volunteer militia was formed, without legal status, as a defence force.

By 1779 the volunteers had ceased to be just a defence force and had become a challenge to the authority of the leading landed interests, the Irish Parliament in Dublin and the English Government in London. During the next decade demands were made for Parliamentary reform, but with the ending of the American war and the return of the regular troops to Ireland, the Volunteer movement declined in number, except in Ulster.

In Ulster, the ideals of the Enlightenment, with its core criticisms of traditional attitudes, customs and morals, were adopted by the Presbyterian middle class. They embraced the Enlightenment principles that human reason could combat ignorance, superstition and tyranny. This in turn led them to challenge the power of the Anglican land-owning and professional class, the so-called Ascendancy. The events of the French Revolution in 1789 led to renewed effort for Parliamentary reform in Ireland. To this end, in October 1791, the Society of United

Irishmen was formed in Belfast to demand reform and the inclusion of all Irishmen in the political life of the country.

However, in France, the Reign of Terror had emerged, sending warning messages about the lack of control. When Britain was drawn into the conflict in 1793, such demands, as perceived by the parliaments of Dublin and London, took on the mantle and image of treason. In the latter parliament, Pitt, the English Prime Minister, decided against granting full Roman Catholic emancipation, a development which was, generally speaking, acceptable to the majority of Ulster Protestants.

Within the province events were moving towards a dangerous climax. Sections of the Protestant and Roman Catholic population were forming themselves into different groups.

At this point it may be useful to clarify the use of the term Protestant. Throughout the 18th century the term was used to refer to those who were members of the established Church of Ireland (Anglican). Presbyterian and other non conformists were known as Dissenters. Therefore, for the sake of simplicity I shall use the term Protestant in its more generic sense as referring to Christian groups separate from the Roman Catholic Church, excluding the Orthodox Churches.

The former grouping became the 'Peep O'Day Boys' and the latter the 'Defenders'. The Defenders adopted secret signs and symbols with biblical references, for example:

Who baptized you?
- St John.
Where?
- At the river.

What river?

- Jordan.

What did he baptize you for?

- To be loyal.

To whom?

- To God and my brethren.

(quoted in Barden, p 225).

In County Armagh both sides were shaping up for the decisive battle which resulted in the creation of the Orange Order. In 1792 a farmer, James Wilson of the Dyan, County Tyrone, started an Orange Club as a defence against the attacks of the Defenders. He appealed for others to join together in the defence of the realm by placing a call to arms in the Belfast News Letter, 1st February 1793. In 1794, according to Sibbett, he attended a meeting of Masonic lodges in Benburb and asked for their assistance in defending against the attacks of the Defenders. They refused, for reasons unspecified, and he swore to 'light a star in the Dyan which would eclipse them forever'.

In September 1795 the Defenders faced the Peep O' Day Boys near Loughall at the Diamond. According to William Blacker, on 21st September the Defenders attacked the house of Dan Winter and were faced with strong opposition. They retreated, leaving many dead and wounded. Events then moved rapidly, in that a decision was taken to form a defensive association and in the house of James Sloan, in Loughall, 'numbers' or warrants were issued for orange lodges. No 1 fell to the Dyan Lodge in Tyrone (see *The Formation of the Orange Order, 1795-1798*, edited papers of Colonel William Blacker and Colonel Robert H. Wallace, p 16).

Blackler adds that nearly all the Dyan members were Presbyterians and the men from Loughall were nearly all Anglicans (Episcopalians). Thus we have clear evidence that the order had a wide appeal within the Protestant community. Consequently, the Order spread rapidly through the rest of the province, with the members pledging allegiance to the Crown and Constitution founded by William III, the Prince of Orange.

There is reasonably strong evidence that these early Orange organisations had a ritual of initiation (see HRAPO p 26 for a fuller discussion), eg in evidence to the House of Lords Select Committee on the State of Ireland 1825, the Grand Secretary of Armagh, the Very Rev Dean Holt Waring, said in relation to signs and passwords used by the Order:

'There was one in 1795; added to again in 1797; another in 1802; there was another in 1820; another in 1825. The first question was:

From whence came you?
-From the House of Bondage.
Whither do you go?
- To the promised land.
How do you expect to get there?
- By the benefit of a password.
Have you that password?
- I have.
Will you give it to me?
- I will divide it with a brother.

Changes of this nature were most likely a guard against

betrayal. The outward sign for an Orangeman was an Orange ribbon. Dewar adds that the degree of Orange Marksmen had been added in 1796 (p 106) and that a person could wear a ribbon of orange, purple and blue.

Although it is possible that after 1795 the earlier Boyne Society was incorporated into the new Orange Order, it is also possible that it continued as a separate organisation in County Armagh for the next 50 years or so (see HRAPO p 11). In 1798 the Antrim Grand Lodge adopted for its own use the Rules and Regulations of the Boyne Society, and these in turn became the basis of the rules of the Grand Lodge of Ireland.

CHAPTER THREE

THE ORDERS OF KNIGHTHOOD

Any attempt to discuss the history of organisations of knighthood, such as the Knights of St John (the Knights of Malta) and the Knights Templar, must first deal with the issue of historical legitimacy of origin. This is a difficult task when, in some cases, such a lineage is not easy to establish. Additionally, some of these organisations are, to all intents and purposes, the creation of private individuals or groups. For example, the 18th and early 19th centuries witnessed the emergence of the Order of Saint Joachim, the Order of the Holy Sepulchre of Jerusalem and the Order of the Temple of Jerusalem.

The majority of these self-styled orders failed to outlive their founders. The order of the Knights, which this study will deal with, emerged in the 12th century. In this period the Knights of St John of Jerusalem, the Knights Hospitaller and the Knights Templar emerged. To all intents and purposes these orders and many others, such as the Teutonic Knights and the Knights of Christ, were bound into the religious and monastic vows of the early Roman Catholic Church.

In the case of the Knights of St John of Jerusalem, their origins would appear to be the consequence of the actions of a group of merchants from Amalfi, Italy. In the eleventh century they founded a hospice in Jerusalem, near the Holy Sepulchre. The siege of Jerusalem forced it to close, but it later reopened under the direction of Brother Gerard. The order became a military one, probably around the 1130s, and formed a community under the rule of St Augustine. However, even these events are clouded with complexity in the various available historical accounts. Some say that St John the Baptist was the patron of the Hospitallers and that the foundation, as laid by Gerard, was under Benedictine rule rather than that of St Augustine.

In his book *Knights of Malta: Ancient and Modern* (1903), T H Gilmour claimed that the knights in question were known as the Knights Hospitallers of St John (The Almoner) of Jerusalem. Their patron was St John Eleemon (The Almoner).The son of Epiphanius, Governor of Cyprus. He was the Patriarch of Alexander in the seventh century. He created a fraternity in Jerusalem in order to nurse the infirm and wounded pilgrims and was canonised as St John of Jerusalem. In their history of the Knights of Malta published in 1915, Rembower and Gray claimed that the hospital of St John the Almoner was the 'cradle of the Order' (p 6).

In another work on the topic, *The Knights of Malta*, H J A Sire claimed that the hospice was dedicated to St John the Baptist with a lay fraternity under the Augustine Rule. The official website of the Roman Catholic Order of Malta claims that under a Papal Bull of 15 February 1113, Pope Paschal II sanctioned the establishment of the Hospitallers order dedicated to St John the Baptist. (Rembower and Gray add that he exempted them from payment of tithes and gave the Hospitallers the privilege of electing their own Superior, P 8). According to Gilmour, in III3 Pope Paschal II granted the Order freedom from authority, spiritual or temporal. This ended the rule of the Pope over the Order. Some light (or darkness!) is shed on this issue in an article entitled *Torphichen and the Knights Hospitaller*, by W J MacLennon, Professor Emeritus at the University of Edinburgh, in which he points out that the hospital was established by the merchants when under the charge of Gerard and adopted the Benedictine Rule. In 1120 the next superior called himself Grand Master of the Order of St John of Jerusalem and changed the rule to that of St Augustine.

After the fall of Jerusalem to the Muslims in 1189 the Order retreated to Margat and then to Acre. When the latter fell in 1291 they moved to Cyprus, then to Rhodes, probably around 1310, and later inherited the estates in the Levant of the Templars who had been abolished in 1312. Earlier, in 1301, the Order had been organised into seven Langues or Tongues: Provence, Auvergne, France, Spain, Italy, England and Germany. These Langues corresponded to regional groupings of priories, which in turn were grouped into commanderies. Gilmour offers the following, slightly different, sub-divisions: Provence, Auvergne, France, Italy, Aragon, England, Germany and later Castile. (England included Scotland and Ireland; Castile included Portugal and Leon). The governing body of each division was called a Grand Priory and the chief official the Grand Prior, with the supreme council being called the Chapter General and the head official the Grand Master.

In 1522 the Turks forced the Order out of Rhodes and as a result of the actions of the Emperor and King of Spain, Charles V, they found a home in Malta. From Malta they developed into a powerful seagoing force and became an obstacle in the path of Muslim advance. It was on Malta that the battle known as the Great Siege took place. The eventual victory of the defenders led to the decline in the Muslim threat to Europe. In 1571 the Order's fleet joined with warships from Italy and Spain and at the Battle of Lepanto it routed the Muslim threat in the Mediterranean. These events reflected the fact that the Knights of Malta were now one of the strongest military and naval powers of the period.

However, across Europe, what had started as a broad religious revival split Christianity. The Protestant Reformation had begun to take root, particularly in Germany, Switzerland, Holland, Scotland and England. Inevitably divisions occurred within the Order and by the end of the 17th century those Knights who remained on Malta were conquered by Napoleon when he was en route to Egypt. They were expelled from Malta, and it was not until 1834 that they obtained a new base in Rome. They adopted the title Knights of Malta to distinguish themselves from the Protestant Order which had emerged in other parts of Europe.

It is from here that the Roman Catholic branch of the Order maintain their world wide hospitaller movement. It is recognised as an independent country by the Vatican and maintains co called 'embassies' in some countries, though not in the UK, the USA or Canada.

The historical background to the Order in Scotland is complex and confusing. It is very difficult to separate fact, fiction and mythology from the various accounts which deal with this matter. I have been unable to trace some of the quoted historical sources, but I have included these references as they do reflect the level of historical knowledge available at the time these claims were being made.

In Chapter XII of his book, Sire notes that the Order was granted its first possession by David I at Torphichen, but adds that, contrary to the suggestion that this was in 1124, it may have been later. He adds that during his reign, Malcolm I (1153-63) granted them a house in every burgh (p 176). Rembower and Gray claim that a distinctly Scottish branch came into existence in 1163 under David I as Grand Prior or Master (their claim is based upon Proctor's *History of the Crusades*, Thalheimer's *Mediaeval History* and Mill, p 8.) By 1199, when King John came to power, the Order had 28 preceptories in England (Sire, p 177).

In Ireland the situation was quite different. Thanks to the influence of the Anglo-Norman ascendancy and the tutelage of Richard de Clare, Second Earl of Pembroke, otherwise known as Strongbow, the Order received the gift of Kilmainham and it was here that the Priory seat was established. By 1212 the Priory had in its possession some 29 preceptories. During the first half of the fourteenth century the Kilmainham Priory came under the control of Irish families. This lasted until power shifted back to England and Henry VIII imposed control. Kilmainham was surrendered to him in 1540. The Langue in England retained Turphichen and in 1547 it was conferred on Sir James Sandilands. He surrendered it to the crown in 1564 and received it back with the title Lord Torphichen (Sire p 187).

In their book *Knights of St John of Jerusalem*, Cowan, Mackay and Macquarrie point out that into the 16th century the Scottish section of the Order had links to Rhodes and Malta (p xvii). According to them it is not possible to give a clear date regarding the Orders first arrival in Scotland. Their earliest found reference is a list of properties dated 1434 (p xxvi), when it is claimed King

David had given them land in Torphichen and other land had been given to them by King Fergus in Galway. Throughout the 14th century evidence of the Order is scarce. However they make references to King Robert the Bruce conferring land etc on the Order, dated 1314. The master of the Order was Ralph or Rodolph Lindsay at least in 1356-7.

In 1356 the Pope recommended master David de Mar, procurator of the Master and Brethren of the Hospital of St John of Jerusalem, to transact business in Scotland. As a result of the Great Schism within Christianity the Hospitallers in Scotland supported the Avignon Pope after 1388 until 1418 (p xxxviii) when the schism was resolved. During this century William Knollis obtained a grant of the preceptory until 1510. (Rembower and Gray add that as far back as 1463 the Knights had contact with the English and Scottish knights under Grand Master Knolls p 15). He is succeeded by George Dundas (p xlvii) but things did not go smoothly and for the next decade his right to hold office was disputed. It was not until 1518 that he was firmly installed (p 1). He was succeeded by Walter Lindsay c 1532/3. Then Sandilands of Calder in 1541 when he was granted ancienitas of Torphichen (p lii). This was confirmed by the Pope when Lindsay died in 1546. For a fuller discussion see pp xviii-liv.)

Sir James Sandilands was born circa 1511 in Calder, Scotland. In December 1540 he was received into the Order and in 1541, as indicated above, the Grand Master de Homedes gives the *ancienitas* (the right of expectancy) to him for the preceptory. After Lindsay died he took over at Torphichen, which was confirmed by the Pope in June 1547, and in 1550 he was invested by the spiritual and temporal powers attendant to the position in a ceremony presided over by a knight of the French Langue, Peter Ourrier (see Cowan, Mackay and Macquarrie p 11). In February 1563 or 1564 he resigned all the property belonging to the Hospitallers in Scotland into the hands of the monarchy and as a consequence became the hereditary baron of Torphichen. By the end of 1564, although some Roman Catholic knights had connections with the Knights of Malta in Scotland, the recruitment and revenue base had gone (ibid p liv). At this juncture Cowan et al infer that the Order ceased to exist in Scotland.

However Gilmour, the official historian of the Knights of Malta, develops the progress of the Order along the following lines. In his book *Chapter VI - the Sixth Language*, he emphasises that, as the writ of Henry VIII did not run in Scotland, there was no necessity to suppress the Order, as it was Protestant.

Central to this claim is the central role and influence of Sir James Sandilands in the formation of the Order. Gilmour says he was converted by John Knox in 1553 and quotes from McCrie's *The Life of John Knox* (D D Knox's History of Scotland and State Papers), in which it appears that Knox stayed at Calder House, the seat of the Sandilands, and that the latter was a friend of the Reformed faith and had supported its preservation in Scotland. (Rembower and Gray, using as their evidence *Vide Vertot's Historie des Chevaliers Hospitalers de S. Jean de Jerusalem et Enc. Brit*, say that Protestant Knights had deserted to Scotland and England in 1557.)

In 1572, David Seaton, along with other Scottish Knights, separated themselves from the Reformed fraternity and went to Germany. In 1643, the Order was reintroduced into Ireland to protect Protestants during the rebellion. This was the second Grand Priory in Ireland and a branch still existed in 1795 when the Orange and the Black Orders were interconnected. Furthermore, it is claimed that separate warrants were held. In some cases, certain degrees were given under an Orange warrant, while for others it was necessary to apply to a Black lodge.

An examination of a particular document is helpful in clarifying this assertion and subsequent developments. The document is entitled A Report of Proceedings of the Annual Assembly of the Knights of Malta ex in Ireland, held in Dublin 11 April 1850 into the newly instituted Grand Black Chapter of Ireland. The latter had held a meeting in Newry the previous December in which it had referred to 'the existence of a spurious Black Lodge in Ireland' adding a caution to 'all Knights of the Black Order in Ireland against holding any intercourse with any member or members of any spurious Black Lodge in Ireland'. Although this report is extremely wordy and full of classical and biblical references, I feel that the following points are a true reflection of the issues discussed.

In relation to the claim that the Knights of Malta are spurious. The report goes onto to say that up to 1835 they were all alike in terms of ceremonies and lectures but after that year the Grand Master of the Orange Order dissolved the Institution in England. It goes on 'Does the 'Chapter' hold our succession 'spurious' for want of illustrious ancestors? What nobler ancestry than the Scottish reformers and the French Protestants can the world furnish?... Was it ignorant of its own origin and of the facts which caused it to be loosened from the parent assembly in Scotland?' (p 8). It adds 'New lectures have been promulgated: surely the initiated will observe the glaring departures from the original and immutable landmarks of the Order' (p 8).

According to the report, the Scottish background of the Order is as follows: In 1120 King David the First founded St John's Preceptory in Linlithgowshire. In 1463, the honour of ordination was conferred on Sir William Knolls by the Grand Master at Rhodes. Sir George Dundas was his successor and then Sir William Lindsay. In 1538 Sir James Sandilands was in charge and went on to claim that 'his love for evangelical Christianity was such that he built a Presbyterian church on the site of one of the wings of the Preceptory' (p 11): John Knox resided (at Sandilands house): 'the first sacrament of the Supper given in Scotland, after the Reformation was dispensed in (this house).' (p 11). Gilmour acknowledges that this dating is in conflict with that given by McCrie but doesn't dwell on the contradiction (p 5).

The report (p 12) refers to a *History of the Inquisition* by Llorente, which, the writers say, implies the existence of two distinct orders of Knights of Malta, one Masonic and the other not, with secret systems of initiation. The Report claims that some of the brethren associated with the 'Chapter' admit that the Grand Lodge in Scotland is their *alma mater* but that 'in consequence of purchase and treaty, its authority was transferred to Ireland'. This latter claim is denied by the authors of the Report in the following terms: 'Where (are)...the deed of purchase and transfer ... deposited?' But some may, with more plausibility, argue that the Order existed in Ireland from time immemorial, and that the privilege of opening Lodges without warrant was inherent in themselves. They go on to point to the fact that the Order in Ireland was dissolved by Henry VIII, but not in Scotland. Therefore, we 'hold the chain of transmission' (p 13.) They add (p 14) 'we are the only successors of the Scottish Knights'. They acknowledge that the claim (by the other Order) that 'the Irish Grand Lodge Warrant is in their possession...(may be true)...but the existing proprietors of that Warrant protest against their right to use it.' (p 14.) The report concludes by extending the hand of friendship to the brethren of the 'new' Order but points out that they are a spurious organisation (p 14-15). Later events show that this gesture was found to be unacceptable to the 'new' Order.

To return to Gilmour, on p 60 he claims to be in possession of an undated copy of rules belonging to the Royal Black Association, which appears to go as far back as 1795. These observe that the Order is separate from the Orange Order and notes that membership of it is conditional on a person having travelled the degrees of Orange and Purple. The following declaration must be read by the Master to a candidate prior to initiation: 'Whereas our Christian forefathers, the Knights of Malta... We, the members of the Royal Black Institution, will... imitate their glorious acts.' He draws attention to the fact that this obligation is substantially the same as that of the Knights of Malta and that the opening and closing prayers are identical (p 61.) He adds that the following documents are evidence that the Knights of Malta are the older Order:

- No155, Grand Black Order of Orangemen: Monaghan regiment... dated 30 August 1814.

- A certificate headed with an arch showing the emblems of degrees and colours of orange, purple, black, scarlet, old blue and royal mark, dated 12 June 1816.

- A document headed 'Royal Black Association No 3' and a certificate of 'Brother Sir Thomas Burgess' initiated into (degree)... of a Royal Arch Black Knight Templar' dated 2 March 1821.

- Burgess became a member of No 24 and the document is judged to be from No 3 of the Grand Lodge of Scotland.
- A parchment document issued by a lodge holding its authority from the Grand Black Lodge of Scotland entitled Royal Black Lodge: Honourable Protestant Association: 1st Royal regiment dated August 1829, Bangalore, East Indies. Its colours represent the degrees up to and including the green.

From this evidence, Gilmour argues that the theory that the Grand Lodge of Scotland was founded in 1831 is false (p 64). He then turns to deal with a Grand Lodge Warrant, which he believes implies a reconstruction of some sort, probably necessitated by the introduction of Orangeism into Scotland and the influx of members who were probably Orangemen. He adds that, from this time onwards, the Order in Scotland was closely connected to the Orange Institution. The legitimacy of this reconstruction was based on a letter from the Grand Secretary, on the instructions of the Grand Council, to the Grand Master to produce the authorisation for the reconstruction. This warrant is dated 24 June 1831. He argues that the reconstruction was legal and that Grand Master Donaldson held the letters of authority (p 67).

An additional piece of the historical puzzle is referred to in a book called *The Billy Boys: A Concise History of Orangeism in Scotland* by William S Marshall. In Appendix 1, he claims that the first preceptory of the Royal Black Institution in Scotland was the Ancient Sons of William RBP 118, Glasgow 1856 and that prior to this date it met as Royal Black Lodge No 2 of the Knights of Malta. He uses as his source the Relief of Derry anniversary programme for 1983 of the Provincial Grand Black Chapter of Scotland.

By the 1900s many organisations existed which held claim to

direct links with the original Order. In order to clarify their historical veracity, if only to dismiss them from the following discussion, we must outline some of these claims.

An organisation called the Johanniterorden claims a direct connection with the order of St John, which to be precise is called the Balley Brandenburg of the Knightly Hospital Order of St John of Jerusalem. Its literature says it was recognised by the Pope around 1113 with the double task to fight for the faith and to give service to the Herren Kranken - the respected ill. Around the time of the Reformation its leadership became Lutheran. It was dissolved in 1810 by Friedrich Wilhelm III, King of Prussia, but in 1852 was reintroduced as the Protestant branch of the old Johanniterordens by King Friederich-Wilhelm IV of Prussia. Although it retains the symbol of a red Maltese Cross, it is purely a spiritual order of chivalry and its members have a dual duty - to support the Christian belief and to work on behalf of the needy and those in illness.

In the following discussion I have drawn on the work of Guy Stair Sainty and in particular Appendix IV of his book *The Orders of Saint John* (1991). This particular section is complex, but I feel that the following is an honest reflection of the parts which are relevant to this study.

Firstly, the Russian link which had been suppressed by Czar Alexander I and its supposed revival in 1908 in New York under the title 'The Grand Priory of America of the Sovereign Order of St John of Jerusalem'. It would appear to have collapsed in 1912. (Rembower and Gray claim that Nicholas (?), the Emperor of Russia, had granted the Knights of Malta refuge when other monarchs of Christendom denied them asylum.)

In 1910 an 'Association of the Knights of Malta' emerged, and a year later was recorded by the State of New Jersey as the Association of the Sovereign Order of Saint John of Jerusalem. In 1953 its name was altered to the Sovereign Order of Saint John of Jerusalem Inc. Over the next couple of years schisms appeared within the group and defectors created their own groups or 'orders'.

In the 1920s the Union of Hereditary Commanders and Knights of the Grand Priory of Russia of the Order of Saint John of Jerusalem makes an appearance. It 1972 it renamed itself the Most Sacred Order of the Orthodox Hospitallers, having abandoned the name and cross of St John. However, in 1977, a breakaway grouping became the Sovereign Order of the Orthodox Knights Hospitaller of Saint John of Jerusalem – Former Russian Grand Priory of the Order of Malta in Saint Petersburg.

In Denmark there is the Sovereign Order of the Hospitallers of Saint John of Jerusalem of Denmark, but it is not linked to the Russian grouping and would appear to have been founded in 1934, although it claimed an earlier ancestry. It was more a private organisation with the status of a charity. In 1954 would-be knights could be admitted on payment of a fee.

Over the years from 1960-90 a variety of groupings emerged with the titular link to the Knights of St John with 'connections' to the former Yugoslavia and in particular the exiled King Peter II, who lived, at this time, in New York. As there has never been the remotest historical connection with Yugoslavia, I feel that any further discussion is unnecessary.

However, in the case of the USA, the following group emerged: the Sovereign Order of the Hospitallers of Saint John of Jerusalem - Knights of Malta - OSJ Inc, New York 1964. Over the next decade divisions within this group led to various new organisations emerging with similar titles. The most active was the Sovereign Military and Hospitaller Order of Saint John of Jerusalem Knights of Malta United States Priory of the Order of Saint John Knights of Malta Ecumenical. An unrelated Sovereign Military and Hospitaller Order of Saint John of Jerusalem, Ecumenical Knights of Malta, Grand Priory of Castile and Leon and its founder has such a complicated purported history as to be beyond the scope of this study (see Gilmour Chapter 7 p 156).

None of the aforementioned 'orders' would appear to have any connection with the Protestant Knights of Malta referred to by Gilmour and others (an examination and historical outline of the North American connection of this Order will follow later).

Perhaps at this stage, the central notion is, as Sainty points out, that common features of these groupings were that they had a charitable status and that they lacked acceptance by the Roman Catholic Church or any sovereign state. However the necessity for these features is questionable when we now turn to examine the following organisation.

The present-day organisation variously called the Knights Hospitallers of St John of Jerusalem, the Knights of Rhodes or Knights of Malta, is not involved in any charitable deeds along the lines of the aforementioned organisations; it does not seek recognition from the Roman Catholic Church or any sovereign state. It is to all intents and purposes a fraternal Protestant order. These features are the basis of a pamphlet called *The Truth about Black Knighthood*, issued by the Supreme Grand Encampment of Ireland. The development of this organisation in North America during the 19th and 20th centuries can be traced through the writing of Gilmour, the medium of the Annual Reports of the Imperial Parent Grand Black Encampment and various Malta Bulletins from

Pennsylvania, USA, together with some reports in various newspapers of the period.

According to Gilmour, Chapter VII, George Donaldson, Past Grand Master, took to Montreal Canada Warrant No 2 and established a branch of the Order circa 1841-43. Another Knight, Thomas Johnston, installed Warrant No 31 at Hornbytown near Toronto in July 1844. On 24 June 1845 an encampment, Warrant No 4, Toronto, was established. By 1875 the Grand Lodge in Scotland had granted power to issue Warrants and to govern to the Supreme Grand Black Encampment of Toronto, Province of Ontario, British America or New Dominion. In the same year the latter body resolved that the Order in Canada should be open to all Protestants and not confined to members of the Orange Order. At a meeting of the Imperial Grand Encampment, Glasgow, on 23 June 1877, the Supreme Grand Commander of America, Sir Knight R E A Land, thanked the body 'for granting a Kingdom Warrant… (with) power to work it as they thought fit: he was confident they had the foundation of the best Protestant society in America'.

However, not all members of the Order were happy with the new power granted to the Supreme Encampment of America. At a meeting of the Imperial Encampment in Glasgow on 14 December 1878, a Washington Encampment, Philadelphia, complained against the Supreme Encampment for reducing the number of degrees and appealed to the Imperial Encampment to cancel the Supreme Warrant and expel the Officers.

On 14 June 1879, the Imperial ruled that the Supreme had gone too far in removing the degrees. In relation to admitting non-Orange Protestants, it ruled that this was never a fundamental principle of the Order, only a byelaw, and that this practice could continue. Gilmour points out that this ruling was in conflict with the General Qualifications, ie 'Any person seeking admission… must at the time of this admission be a member of the Loyal Orange Society and have received the degrees of Orange and Arch purple'.

By the 5th June 1880 the Supreme Encampment had expelled several encampments for questioning their right to reduce the 'Ritualistic' work of the Order and the Imperial Encampment felt duty bound to support their actions. (It is unclear which degrees are involved, as Gilmour does not elaborate on this point.)

However, the issue over the degree structure was causing ripples far beyond the Americas. At a meeting of the Grand Priory of Ireland on 3rd June 1880, disquiet was expressed at the possibility of reducing the degrees to 8 and 'That we… appoint and instruct a deputation… to oppose by every legitimate means any intended innovation as ruinous to us, injurious to the entire Institution and which would degrade us in the estimation both of the Black Chapter and the world, as recent legislation has already done'.

Pressure from the Irish Knights led to the cancellation of the Warrant of the Supreme Encampment of America in 1881. This led to a split in the Americas, one section following the ruling of the Parent Encampment and the other following an independent path. Eventually, at the annual Convocation of the Imperial Encampment, 10th June 1882, Companion Richard J Irwin, Constantine Encampment, Philadelphia, had conferred on him the degrees suppressed by the Supreme Encampment. Thus once again all the degrees were worked in America. Such tensions, I believe, are highlighted in the following correspondence.

A letter in my possession from a Companion Worshipful Master Adair of No 45 Pittsburgh, Star of the West, 1st November 1883, to the Supreme Commander of Ireland, James Ledgerwood, enquires about an organisation calling itself the Irish Black Preceptor. He adds that he and other Knights are having a hard fight in the city against them. Also, that the Grand Orange Lodge there had passed a motion condemning the Knights of Malta and recognising the Irish Black.

On 9th June1884 the Supreme Encampment of America was revived and permission was given to create an Order of Merit - the Great Cross of Malta degree. In 1889 a union took place between the Imperial Black Encampment and the Supreme Commandery of America dated 1st June and ratified in Glasgow on 15th June 1889. It would appear that this union was not wholly successful, as some encampments of the breakaway group from 1881, when the Supreme Warrant was cancelled, still conferred a few degrees. They call themselves the Chapter General of the Order of Knights of Malta, but in Scotland they are referred to the Land Party. Another schism takes place in June 1889 when some Knights, who had belonged to Jerusalem Commandery, No 37, Philadelphia, joined with a Charles McClintock, of Constantine Commandery No1, creating an organisation calling itself the American and Independent Order of Knights of Malta. Because its initials were the same as the Ancient and Illustrious Order of Knights of Malta, many people were deceived. To end this deception a ruling was made in law in the Court of Common Pleas, Philadelphia, forbidding the use of the bogus title on 1st December 1900.

Confirmation of these developments is to be found in a report in the New York Times of 6 January 1890, under the heading 'Rivals In Their Order':

'A meeting took place between the Grand Chapter of New York and the Grand Commandery of the Ancient and Illustrious Knights of Malta to discuss the question as to which group was the real representative of the Order. This report confirms that the Order spread from Toronto to

New York around 1875, when the first encampment is established. The issues of a purely Protestant Order and the number of degrees were discussed in the following manner. Firstly, the Order was originally Protestant and in Great Britain a condition of membership was that a candidate had to be a Royal Arch Purple Orangeman. Although the American Knights were all Protestant it was felt that intolerance was distasteful in America and that as a consequence that portion of the principles was removed by the Chapter General. Also because the degree structure was found to be difficult it was reduced from 12 to 8 and then to 4. The followers of the old ritual of Scotland claimed that the Chapter General had no authority to make these decisions and consequently had been disenfranchised by the Imperial Black Encampment. The discussion turned heated and a squad of policemen had to intervene between the two factions and the meeting broke up in disorder.'

The report concludes with a statement by the Grand Commander of the Knights of Malta (old ritual) to the effect that New York had 13 Commanderies with a total membership of about 2000 and that the other faction was small in numbers.

The annual reports of the Imperial Parent Grand Black Encampment show the following developments in Order in America. In the Report from the Grand Inspector General of America Chicago, dated 1886, the following Commanderies (encampments) are working:

Numbers:
26. St Elmo, Rochester NY
27 Washington, Philadelphia Pa
29 Philadelphia
44 Mount Calvary, Wilmington, Del

45 Star of the West, Pittsburgh Pa

46 Olive Branch, Albany NY

48 Phoenix, Troy, NY

51 Montgomery, Norristown, Pa

53 Eureka, Black River, Mich

56 Palestine, Chicago, Ills

The number of Commanderies working is listed as follows:

1894 - 150

1895 - 168

1899 - 259

1900 - 292

1902 - 325

1914 - 276

1925 - 414

1929 - 395

1930 - 383

1931 - 364

1932 - 354

1933 - 323

In 1929 a reference was made to the desire of the Supreme Commandery in America to divide the Order into (a) the Commandery with only Knight Hospitaller and the Knight of Malta and (b) the Council with the other 10 degrees. This was agreed upon by the Imperial Council.

The Order would appear to have declined in numbers over the next half century or so. Its strongest locations had been in the states of Pennsylvania, New York and Utah.

CHAPTER FOUR

THE ROYAL BLACK INSTITUTION AND THE KNIGHTS OF MALTA

The background to the emergence of the Royal Black Institution (RBI) and the decline in influence and status of the Knights of Malta (also referred to as the Scotch Black) are difficult to disentangle from the available literature, some of which is clearly partisan. In relation to the Knights of Malta the major source remains Gilmour's work, so I have decided to start with his contribution. He refers to an application on 24 March 1834 from Ballymacarret, Belfast, and infers from the information in the letter that those requesting a warrant had been working under an Irish Warrant. The warrant was granted, No 28, in the name of a John Darby. This decision, he says, is the beginning of many problems with Ireland. In June 1834 the Grand Lodge (Knights of Malta) in Glasgow demanded that a William Fossett face a trial by the Master and members of No 28 for violating the rules of the Scottish Lodge, adding that a Robert Plunkett was also to be expelled for selling Warrant No 7.

In the August of the same year a letter from William Fawcett (spelt Fossett in previous letters) answers the charges made against him. He points out that he bought No16 Warrant, issued by the Grand Black Lodge of the city of Dublin 1 February 1822 and had in his possession the lodge seal plus other articles, adding that he had intended to have the warrant renewed by the Scottish body but had been informed that he was 'excluded'. A later report to the said body in September 1834 vindicated him and made the recommendation that the Grand Lodge grant him the renewal.

Gilmour goes into great detail regarding the chaotic state of Irish affairs over the next decade or so in which warrant holders lose touch with Scotland, problems with the Orange Order arise over the higher degrees and the selling of warrants and the holding of illegal meetings take place. On p 80, he quotes from correspondence dated 3 March 1846 from a James Hadden, Master of No 2 Killyman to the Scottish Grand Lodge regarding the creation of a Grand Lodge in Ulster (Coleraine). According to Gilmour this is the first reference to the creation of what later became the Grand Black Chapter of Ireland (RBI), p 81.

On p 84, he lists the following as connections of the Knights of Malta to the Orange Institution:

1814 Grand Black Lodge of Orangemen

1816 Loyal Orange Associations (new system)

1822 proof of the Second Grand Lodge when they issued Warrant No 16 (no proof of existence after this date).

1834 the Scottish Grand Lodge issues warrants in Ireland

1844 Grand Lodge of Ireland resuscitated (designation Grand Lodge No 3 in Ireland but divisions continue to exist).

Referring back to the events of 1846, he argues that if the desire for a Grand Lodge to unite all divisions had been honourable towards the Grand Lodge of Scotland there would have been one body with each Grand Lodge governing its own kingdom but linked to one fraternity. He adds on p 85 that in Armagh an illegal self-appointed body assembled, not one of whose members had received their degrees from the Grand Black Chapter of Ireland, as it did not exist. Out of this meeting emerged a Grand Lodge, later referred to as the Grand Black Chapter of Ireland. This new body excommunicated the Scottish parent body and discarded the Knight of Malta degree - the degree conferred by Grand Lodge No 2 in Ireland from which the Black Chapter descended. Gilmour quotes the following from a old copy of rules belonging to the Royal Black Association (of Ireland) the following codes of rules to be read to candidates prior to initiation, " Whereas our Christian forefathers the Knights of Malta, We, the members of the Royal Black Institution, will imitate their glorious acts and achievements p 60.

On 11 April 1850 the Grand Lodge No 3 met in Dublin to examine the state of affairs (p 86); this was the last known meeting.

On p 89 he points out that the Grand Lodge of Scotland was still granting warrants in Ireland in 1861 and 1867. The Provincial Grand Lodge of Ulster was granted to a William Stewart in Belfast. In 1874 it was superseded when a Kingdom Warrant was granted to James Ledgerwood in Belfast.

Aiken McClelland, the Orange and Black historian, also a Freemason, refers in his book on the life of William Johnston of Ballykilbeg to some of the aforementioned events. In Chapter 3 he assumes that the Grand Black of Knights of Malta (Scotland) was similar to the Masonic Order, but Roman Catholics were not admitted, claiming that members were unwarranted or hedgemasons. In 1796 some Loughall Orangemen added a new degree, the Plain Purple, and over a period of some 20 years the Orange Order, under the influence of those members who were either Knights of Malta or Freemasons, created a number of degrees.

When the Grand Orange Lodge was dissolved in 1836 some former Orangemen joined organisations such as the Royal Black Association of Orangemen, the Grand Black Order of Orangemen and the Loyal Black Association (the Knights of Malta), the latter being a branch of the parent Scottish body.

If we pause at this juncture, it is obvious that we have conflicting titles for perhaps the same organisations, for example Gilmour speaks of a Grand Black Lodge of Orangemen (1814) and McClelland of the Royal Black Association of Orangemen, the Grand Black Order of Orangemen and the Loyal Black Association. It is probably safe to assume that this latter group is the same as Gilmour's Grand Black Chapter of Ireland p 85 (note that on p 72 the word Lodge is used instead of Chapter). Unfortunately I am unable to link or connect the other titles in a meaningful manner.

So to move to the events of 1846. Some members of the Knights of Malta (the Loyal Black Association of Scotland), desiring independence from the influence of the Scottish Knights of Malta, founded the Grand Black Chapter of Ireland. On 1st March 1847 this newly formed Chapter met members of the Grand Black Order and the Grand Black Lodge of Ireland with 'the purpose of amalgamating the difference and concentrating the forces and sinews of three contending parties each bearing the name of grand lodge... all gave way to the proper feeling, that there should be one head, one mind and one ruling body' (McClelland, p 193). Once again he uses slightly different titles from the previous ones, but one can assume they are the same orders.

McClelland offers the following explanations for the amalgamations:

1. The Grand Orange Lodge of Ireland was reconstituted in 1846.
2. There were fears that the body would crush a smaller body but that a larger one would be a more difficult proposition (p 193).

As to the origins of the hostility of the Orange leaders to the higher degrees, he offers three reasons. First, in order to control its members the Grand Lodge needed to publicly define the memberships terms and its principles. Second, they viewed the higher degrees as a challenge to the legal status of the Orange Order (why this was so is not clarified). Third, some of the degrees were perceived as ridiculous and they annoyed the gentry and the Dublin professionals who made up the Grand Lodge membership (no clarification is offered on this point).

He then examines the basis of the quarrel between the Grand Orange Lodge and the newly formed Grand Black Chapter (the GBC). His suggestion is that it is a mystery, but the most likely explanations are as follows. It was Johnston's hope that the GBC could be modelled on Masonic lines with a pyramid structure, with successively fewer members in the higher degrees, the membership of the last degree to consist of himself and a few friends. Johnston was forced to drop this plan and make all the degrees open to all members of the Royal Black Institution. In a diary entry Johnston says that the 3rd Earl of Enniskillen (the Orange Grand Master) came to try to extinguish the Black (Institution). He added that he promised to have a paper ready by May which would totally separate the two institutions in appearance, to which the Grand

Master expressed complete satisfaction. However, the Grand Black Lodge had already decided, at a special meeting held in December 1862, to seek legal advice on the following questions: Are the Rules legal? Do the Rules, as at present framed, connect the Black Association with the Orange Institution? (As evidence he quotes a report of the meeting of Grand Black Chapter of Ireland held in Orange Hall, Belfast, 30 December 1862 p 2.)

When the Grand Lodge met in May 1863 Johnston submitted the legal opinion and it was agreed that the Black Institution was separate from the Orange Institution. The matter was allowed to lapse.

In an article in the Journal of the Royal Society of Antiquaries of Ireland, Volume 98 Part 2 1968, on the origins of the Imperial Black Chapter of the British Commonwealth, McClelland adds very little of substance to the Johnston material. However, he quotes the following from the evidence given by Stewart Blacker, Grand Secretary of the Grand Orange Lodge of Ireland, to the Royal Commission 1835, on the question of the origins of the Black Lodges:

'I have not the slightest idea but imagine they arose from the desire of the lower orders (in society) to have something more exciting or alarming in the initiation of members; I think it may be a mixture of freemasonry, with that of the old Orange system... originating in the strong desire that vulgar minds... manifest for awful mysteries and ridiculous pageantry.' (p 194.)

The other important contributor to this debate is Edward Rogers, historian of the Orange and Black Institutions, Armagh County Librarian, District Master of Armagh and County Grand Secretary, Deputy Grand Master of the Grand Lodge of Ulster and the first Grand Registrar of the Black Institution after 1846.

Unfortunately, his accounts of events are in conflict with both

Gilmour and McClelland. In his History of the Royal Black Institution, dated 1857, for example, on p 2, he claims that the independence of the Institution dates from 1819-20, when in the former year the District of Armagh determined that meetings of Knights of the different Orders take place on the 1st January and the 1st July in each year, 1820. Also that the Grand Black Order of Orangemen had now arrived in a mature state, referring to a warrant dated 16 September 1797 in the name of the Magnanimous and Invincible Order of Royal Blackmens Association.

The earliest Gilmour reference is 1814 (p 61, Rogers) continues as follows: in 1823 the Grand Lodge had issued 25 warrants (Gilmour makes no reference to these claims in his book). He adds that unfortunately the books and other literature of the Society had been lost or destroyed for the period up to 1834. Gilmour (p 61-67) refers to various warrants operating in the period, eg No 155, Grand Black Order of Orangemen; Monaghan Regiment 1814; Loyal Orange Association, New System, No 155 with degrees including orange, black, scarlet, old blue and royal mark 1816; Royal Black Association, with references to Royal Arch Black Knight Templar 1821; Royal Black Lodge Honourable Protestant Association; 1st Royal Regiment 1829, with degrees up to and including green; Ancient St Johns, Glasgow No 24 1829; and a Grand Lodge Warrant dated 1831 Glasgow.

Rogers continues that in 1834 the Grand Lodge (not to be confused with the aforementioned Grand Lodge) had new officers and a year later the paper trail (my words) of the Society more or less disappears for about 10 years. But according to Gilmour, p 71 ff, the Knights of Malta continued to dispense warrants and confer degrees in Ireland.

At this juncture Rogers starts to examine the Knights of Malta. He suggests that some people 'no doubt taking advantage of the general apathy... introduced into Glasgow an Order... the Knights of Malta... calling themselves the Parent Grand Black Lodge of the Universe'. He points out that he and others can find no evidence for such an order prior to 1835, suggesting that if it had existed, a B. Motherwell of Glasgow and others, in their evidence before the Enquiry of 1835, would have referred to its existence. Motherwell was giving evidence on behalf of the Imperial Grand Orange Lodge of Great Britain and nowhere in his answers or statements is he questioned regarding other orders or organisations.

Rogers then enters into an *ad hominem* attack on a group of Irish Orangemen who, he claims, had fled to Glasgow to avoid the police and in Glasgow had established a Grand Lodge 'composed of men of the lowest grades in society... they proceeded to confer degrees'. He then attacks the creation, in England, of the Grand Britannic Institution and the Grand Council of the Most Noble Order of the Knights of Malta. He adds that both conferred 'Popish Degrees', eg Apron, Sword and Star, Star and Garter, Link and Chain, Knights Templar and Mediterranean Pass.

However, a publication entitled the Rules and Regulations of the Royal Arch Purple and Black Association, Belfast, printed at the Protestant Journal Office 1846, refers to the Knights of Malta (p 11) as 'our Christian forefathers' and says 'We associate to carry out the sublime Mysteries and Secrets of our forefathers, the Knights of Malta' (p 10). So the situation is not nearly as clear cut as Rogers would have us believe.

Gilmour, in Chapter 5 of his book, dealing with the issuing of the first warrant to England, claims that the Imperial Grand

Encampment (Scotch Black) in a correspondence dated 1842 refers to a Joseph Brown (Liverpool) applying for a warrant, but there is no record as to whether or not it was granted. He refers to a letter from the Imperial Grand to a G L Curless of Manchester, Master No 1 dated 24 December 1845, making a reference to 'Britannic' Manchester. A year later, on 18 February 1846, a William Curless, Manchester No 1, wrote to the Imperial Grand mainly about illegal warrants operating in Liverpool. In 1854 the Provincial Grand Priory of England was created, but two years later they reverted back to the control of the Imperial Grand.

By 1868 eight encampments operated in England. In June 1876 a Provincial Grand Priory was granted, but in 1877 reference is made to a Grand Encampment operating illegally in Liverpool and the *Belfast Weekly News* and *Belfast Telegraph* carried notices pointing out that these warrants were cancelled by the Grand Council (p 93) signed Alexander Kennedy IGR. 1877. Gilmour refers to a report dated June 1877 from the Provincial Grand Priory which shows 13 encampments working in England. By 1895 they had been reduced to four and as the situation with the Provincial Grand was fraught with problems (it is unspecified as to why they were in rebellion) the warrants were cancelled and only two reissued under Scottish jurisdiction.

In the History of the Royal Arch Purple Order (pp 122-23) there are references to the Royal Britannic Association of the Knights of Israel in 1904, and degrees of Lieutenant of the Temple and Captain of the Temple (Knights Templar). The degree of Mediterranean Pass could not be revived, as it was lost. The authors of this history quote from the official historian of the Grand Orange Lodge of England that as far as he was aware the Association no longer existed after perhaps 1931 (p 122). It would appear safe to assume that this organisation was the same as the one referred to by Rogers and Gilmour. The earliest reference I can find to this organisation is the following exchanges in evidence to the Royal Commission, 1835.

The Rev James Harris, a member of the Order for some 10-12 years and a member of Church of England (p 116), comments:

2432: When I had seen soldiers in an Orange Lodge, it is not exactly in an Orange Lodge, but in a society growing out of Orangeism that is, in the Brittanic Society.

Q. Is that an offshoot of Orangeism?

A. I would say it is an older society than Orangeism, but it has been lately revived.

Later:

Q. What is the Brittanic Society?

A. I do not know how to answer that question.

Q. Are you a member?

A. I am: it is a society which is called the Loyal Brittanic Society; you may judge of the feelings of the persons that constitute it, when I state that it is very similar to that of Orangeism. I think that will satisfy the Committee, without any further particulars.

Later:

Q. Were you a founder of it?

A. No, it was one of the oldest societies in England.

(Unfortunately this point was not elaborated upon).

Later:

Q. You stated that the objects were the same with those of the Orange Society.

A. They were pretty similar: it is a society very prevalent in Ireland, much more so than Orangeism.

Later:

Q. Are those [in Ireland] called the Brittanic Lodges?

A. No, not that I know of; they are called the Brittanic Institution.

Later:

Q. Have you different signs and passwords in the Brittanic Society from the Orange ?

A. Yes.

Q. Is every member of the Brittanic Lodge, to which you are attached as grand chaplain, a member of the Orange Lodge?

A. Yes, he must be or have been an Orangeman....

Q. Is it thus connected with the Orange Society?

A. No, it has no connection with it; though it refers to it.

In evidence from Mr Chatwoode. Deputy Grand Secretary, Loyal Orange Institution of Great Britain.

2333 ff: referring to the Brittanic Society:

In fact it is a mere nothing in its nature; it is merely that some, chiefly of the lower orders have a fancy to have an occasional social meeting of persons who have been or are in the Orange Society. Later:

2552. These are persons who continue what they call orders that are not recognised by the Orange Society: what some would consider nonsensical orders. The Orange Society does not recognise those orders at all.

Further light is shed on this organisation in a report in the Belfast Weekly News, dated 24/05/1906, which carried the following references. It is claimed that in 1820 the Grand Orange Lodge in Ireland forbade the giving of degrees above the Purple and that out of this situation emerged the Grand Black Orange Lodge (in Ireland) and in England the Royal Britannic Association was created. The report goes on to say that up to 1835 they were alike in terms of ceremonies and lectures but after the events of 1835, the Grand Master of the Orange Order dissolved the Institution in England.

In Huddersfield in 1836, an English Grand Lodge was established. This organisation proceeded to grant warrants under the title Grand Protestant Confederation. In this period the Royal Britannic Association ceased to exist as a Grand Lodge in England. The report adds that in Ireland, during the period 1836-46, all the orders and degrees above Purple were lost and new ones had to be manufactured. The degrees of the Sword and Star and Knight Templar (Lieutenant and Captain) were also lost. At this juncture enquiries were made (it does not say to whom) regarding the working of a Knight Templar of St John of Jerusalem encampment. A committee of six was set up to look into the matter and on 7 October 1905, in Bacup, they decided not to accept the title Royal Britannic Association, which included, above the Captain degree, the Mediterranean Pass, a lost degree in England. From this meeting emerges the Knight Templar of Loyal Orangemen. A warrant is devised to represent all the various degrees and orders.

The meeting closed with a vote of thanks for guidance to the Grand Geometrician of the Universe (a reference more in keeping with Freemasonry!). The warrant is accepted.

The Grand Secretary of the Orange Lodge of England, who has been helpful in my research, has recently sent me a copy from a rule book of the Royal Britannic Association of Knights of Israel, dated 1931, in which it claims to have emerged from the Orange Institution and that its degrees are those of the 'Higher degrees of Orangeism' and that after 1822 it became a distinct and independent order. It lists the degree as follows:

Scarlet.
Royal Arch Marksman.
Blue or Priestly Order.
White.
Gold.
Black or Knightly Order.
Green or knights of the Red Cross.
Apron.
Sword and Star.
Lieutenant of the Temple.
Captain of the Temple.

The clear overlap between the names of these degrees of the Orders is a feature of all the correspondence I have read. One is led to the conclusion that they have a common source and that this source was and is Freemasonry. This theme will be developed further in the next chapter, when I examine the whole question of the so called Higher Degrees. (Speculation as to the origin of the degrees of Masonry is outside the scope of this book.)

In Ireland some members give 'the Orders' under an Orange Warrant and others became linked to the Scotch Black. In 1842, in County Down, a Grand Black Orange Lodge of Ireland was created. A certificate exists, dated 1843, issued by Royal Arch Purple, Blue and Black Associations No 2 Clough, Co. Down with symbols relating to the Scotch Black degree system (see HRAPO P 93 ff for a fuller discussion).

In Gilmour there is a reference to a request for 'a certificate for John McClelland, of Banbridge... who had received the degrees of Black, Mark, Scarlet, Blue and Priestly Order' (p 76).

For the next year or so the situation is somewhat chaotic. But at a meeting of some members in Portadown on 14 September 1845 the Parent Grand Black Lodge of the Universe, from which the present Grand Black Lodge of Ireland emerged, was created. McClelland dates this event to 1846. From this self-selecting body, the Grand Registrar, Rogers was ordered to draw up a book of Rules, Form of Warrants and Certificates. These were submitted and approved at a meeting in March 1847 and the motto 'Tria Juncta in Uno' (three joined in one) was adopted.

May one assume that this referred to the three Black jurisdictions with their different names in Scotland, Ireland and England? Probably not. It is more likely that he is referring to the situation in Ireland, where three separate bodies operated, each claiming to be the Grand Black Orange Lodge.

Rogers, in his *History of the Royal Black Institution, Part 111, The Glasgow Knights of Malta, p 5*, dismisses the Scotch Black in terms of their deeds, reputations and religious professions. He examines the Proclamation of the Order which deals with (a) the historical background of the Knights, (b) their invitation to the Grand Black Chapter of Ireland to meet with the Glasgow Knights, (c) the challenge to prove the existence of a Grand Black Lodge in Ireland prior to 1843 - 44, and, (d) the claim that the Glasgow Black were brought from Malta to Scotland by Knox in 1525.

Rogers argues that in 1525 John Knox was twenty years old and that there is no evidence that he visited Malta. The title Knights of Malta was assumed in 1525 when the island became their home. Furthermore, the Knights were strictly under the control of the Church of Rome. These claims are based on the following sources: Vertot's *History of the Knights of Malta*; Hebjot's *History of the Monastic Orders*; Vattel's *Laws of Nations*; Mosheim's *Ecclesiastial History*; Baromus, Mabillion; M.Paris; Cottigan's *History of the Irish Rebellion and Europedia*.

At this point there is confusion over the date relating to John Knox. Rogers gives 1515 and not 1525 as earlier quoted. This is probably a misprint. He goes on to say that the Knights Hospitaliers were approved in 1120 by Pope Calixtus II. The extracts linking the order with the Roman Catholic Church include:

A. Defence of the Catholic faith

B. Confession to priests

C. Participation in the Mass

D. Veneration of the Virgin Mary and St John the Baptist.

Rogers concludes with an appeal to the conscience of the Glasgow Black asking whether they can still exist as a Protestant organisation and calls for a ' bond of union' to take place. (At this point readers may care to refer to the earlier discussion on links and loyalty to the Roman Catholic Church.) No such reconciliation took place and the two organisations retained their separate identities. So what are we to make of these at times conflicting and at times confusing accounts?

William J. Burke, Supreme Grand Sentinel, Supreme Grand Encampment of Ireland. The Ancient and Illustrious Order of Knights of Malta. Circa 1925.

IN MEMORIAM.

"O! for the touch of a vanished hand,
And the sound of a voice that is still."

Ancient St. John's No. 24.

SIR THOMAS HENRY GILMOUR,

Grand Master.

Died on Sunday, 25th December, 1932.

"He giveth His beloved sleep."

Sir Thomas Henry Gilmour, Grand Master and Historian

MALTA
BULLETIN

**Grand Commandery of Pennsylvania, A. & I. O. K. of M.
and Supreme Commandery, Continent of America**

Vol. XXXXVIII, No. 5   MONTGOMERY, PA., DECEMBER, 1972   A. O. 924

Warrant from the Grand Black Encampment of Scotland to the Supreme Grand
Commandery of America.

Malta Bulletin Warrant dated December 1972

Council Chamber of   Commandery No.

To the Supreme Commander, Officers and Members of the

Supreme Grand Commandery,

Ancient ⚔ Illustrious Order Knights of Malta.

GREETING:---

This is to Certify, That at a stated Convocation of this Commandery,

held _____ 189___, it was voted that Sir _____

be recommended to the Supreme Body for Past Commander's Honors, by reason of his being

the organizer of this Commandery.

Witness our hands and the seal of the Commandery, this _____ day of

_____ A. D. 189___   A. O. 84___.

                                          _____ Sir Knight Commander.

[SEAL.]   _____ Recorder.

GIVE ONE TO THE COMPANION.

SEND ONE TO THE SUPREME RECORDER.

Certificate from the Commandery USA.

Square and compasses carved into stone. Part of the foundation stone
on a masonic hall situated in the centre of Lancaster

THE

Ancient and Illustrious Order

OF

KNIGHTS OF MALTA

ANNUAL RECORD FOR YEAR ENDING JUNE,

ANNO DOMINI 1914. ET ANNO ORDINIS 866.

Issued by Imperial Grand Authority.

GLASGOW:

GRAND RECORDER'S OFFICE, 51 LONDON ROAD.

Knights of Malta annual records

Ancient and Illustrious Order of Knights of Malta.

Great Cross Priory,
No. 4.

Belfast,

.................................194... *A.D.*...........*A.O.*

Sir Knight and Companion,

You are requested to attend a stated Convocation of No. 4 Great Cross Priory, to be held (D.V.) in Knights of Malta Hall, 20 Waring Street, on .... , the........... day of........................... , 194 , at 8 p.m. sharp.

Yours fraternally,

W. Scribe

Special Business:

Request to attend a meeting or 'Stated Convocation'

CHAPTER FIVE

THE PROBLEMS OVER THE HIGHER DEGREE STRUCTURE

Clearly there is an issue over the degree structure as practised by the various organisations. The leaders of the Orange Institution were drawn, in the main, from the nobility and the gentry and they disliked the content of the so-called 'higher degrees', ie those beyond Orange and Purple. Furthermore, they held a low opinion of those Orangemen who wished to 'travel' beyond these two degrees. A clear example of this is to be found in the language and terminology used by the Grand Secretary of the Orange Institution in his evidence to the 1835 Select Committee.

His comments jar somewhat with the fact that the Boyne Society, founded in the 17th century, clearly had a hierarchy of degrees which very likely evolved into those of the Orange Institution and the Royal Black Institution. These degrees or orders were confined to a relatively small number of people (see p 12 HRAPO) - shades of the original intention of William Johnston! The authors of the HRAPO clearly show that the earliest degrees of the Orange Institution included the Orange Marksman, in which members wore a ribbon of Purple, Blue and Orange (pp 36-7, 42-

5). Also a certificate of the Royal Orange Association No 174 (Armagh Regiment) 1814 shows emblems relating to Black, Royal Arch Purple and other degrees (p 49). The same authors make a convincing argument that the Royal Arch Purple degree took on a separate status in 1820 (p 136) although it had been 'worked' as early as 1802 (p 60).

It is unclear why the leaders of the Orange Institution held such a dislike for the higher degree structure. In my opinion a possible explanation may be found in the emerging divisions created by the changing social class structure of the 1750s to 1850s.

The members who were supportive of the higher degrees were mainly drawn from the artisan and merchant classes. I realise that in the absence of a close examination of the religious and political affiliations of this group any conclusion must remain speculative. Nevertheless, in Ulster, the tensions surrounding the constitutional links to England and the economic situation ensured that radicalism was a potent force in the political life of the society. The educational apartheid which excluded Ulster Presbyterians and other Dissenters from the main university, Trinity College, Dublin, forced them to study in Edinburgh and Glasgow where the ideals of the Enlightenment were freely voiced and discussed.

It has been calculated that between 1761-1780 the Irish students at Glasgow University comprised 200 sons of tenant farmers, 77 sons of gentry, 60 merchant sons and 42 sons of clergy (for a fuller discussion see E M Johnston - Link p 43). It would therefore be a fairly safe assumption that the events in Antrim and Down in the latter decades of the 1800s, when the artisans and farmers were involved in political activity, 'reflected the influence of such ideals' (see McFarland p 70). Within this section of society the right to hold one's own thoughts and make decisions gelled into a potent dissenting force whose adherents would not be subservient to the views and wishes of the nobility and gentry. Therefore, a rebellion against the leadership of the Orange Institution with its desire to suppress the 'higher degrees' would be an understandable reaction.

However, this somewhat begs the question as to why did the leadership opposed the degrees? Perhaps it was the content and ritual. Or was it the supposed 'origins' of the degrees? Was the link with the degrees something to do with Freemasonry? In unravelling these issues a useful starting point would be an examination of the content of the degrees. As I have earlier discussed, initiation ceremonies and rituals are as old as mankind. So where can one begin?

A major dissenting factor between the RBI and the Knights of Malta would appear to be the question of whether the degrees should be solely based on biblical themes or should they include references to non-biblical themes? On this issue Edward Rogers, writing in his account of the origins 'of the Order and Degrees of the Black Association' is adamant. He argues that the concept of Black Knighthood is based on the story of Joseph in the Old Testament and his rise under Pharaoh to be the Chief Ruler of Egypt. He connects the Gold degree with the gold ring placed on Joseph's finger and the gold chain around his neck. The Crimson degree he links with the blood of the lamb which was slain at the Passover and sprinkled on the door posts and lintels of the Israelites. At the time he was writing he found the following degrees acceptable:

1. Black, including Crimson and Gold
2. Royal Arch
3. Scarlet

4. White

5. Blue

Thus he discarded the additional RBI degrees, even though they are based on the Bible, along with any degree that he considered to be linked to a Roman Catholic order of chivalry or the Crusaders.

In my discussions with some members of the RBI they emphasised that, in their opinion, the Black or 'higher degrees' had been, up to and around 1835, mainly based on the Bible, but as the Order moved away from its biblical roots, so it took on board the other degrees and themes, perhaps from Freemasonry. In order to test the possibility of such a development and in turn to perhaps explain the origins of the symbolism and degrees of the Boyne Society, it is necessary to examine the situation within Freemasonry in Ireland and Scotland at this time.

Freemasonry had a strong aristocratic basis. Such a situation poses a parallel with the rise of the Orange Institution. The Orange leadership comprised the nobility and the gentry and Freemasonry the aristocracy. While exact figures are not available as to whether or not the Orange leaders were Freemasons, the composition of the 'higher degrees' and their possible Masonic origins raises the question - if they did have such origins is this the basis of the opposition?

Before examining this possibility, an additional factor which needs to be considered is the emergence of the United Irishmen and their connections with certain lodges of Freemasons.

At the first meeting of the Belfast Society of United Irishmen on 14 October 1791, those present included Henry Haslett and William Tenant, merchants and members of Lodge 257. Other lodge members present included William McCracken (brother of

Henry Joy) and George and Thomas Sinclair, whose brother William was a founder of the United Irishmen. Other leading figures, such as Henry Grattan, were members of Dublin Volunteer Lodge and Daniel O'Connell was a member of Lodge 413 Limerick. In Armagh 27 Masonic lodges admitted that some of their members had been United Irishmen and they published a resolution denouncing this practice in the hope of 'wiping away the stigma' (Kenneth L Dawson, *Irish News*, May 20 2003). The Worshipful Master Of Lodge 738, James Reynolds, coined the phrase 'Let every Volunteer company become a lodge of Masons' (A McClelland, *Some Aspects of Freemasonry in the late 18th and early 19th century*). Reports were rife that journalists and artisans were joining lodges. When the house of a James McBride, a Freemason and a United Irishman, who lived near Clady, was raided in 1797, badges were found with Masonic symbols on one side and on the other a call for freedom. In October 1797 the Chief Secretary for Ireland, Thomas Pelham, wrote to the Masonic Grand Master, the Earl of Donoughmore, and other members of the Grand Lodge asking for help in dealing with revolutionaries who were Freemasons. Donoughmore agreed to help and sent a 'loyal' Freemason, Charles McCarthy, to inspect the lodges in the north of Ireland

One of the consequences of this type of action was an amendment to the rules to prohibit the discussion of religious and political issues. With the Act of Union the political situation was somewhat defused and the political connections were weakened. The connections between a group such as the United Irishmen and Freemasonry would have been viewed with disquiet by Protestants in the Orange Institution and may help us to understand the resentment towards the so called 'higher degrees' on the part of 'loyal' members of the latter organisation.

To return to the question of the degree connection with Freemasonry and the issue of the non-biblical roots of these degrees, we need to examine in some detail the composition of these degrees and their possible origins. Without going into the complicated history of Freemasonry, I propose to use the following as a starting point. The Old Charges, which are among the oldest surviving Masonic documents, trace the organisation or Craft to biblical times. They include an opening prayer to God as the Great Architect of the Universe. Other references include an orientation to the Old Testament; Solomon's Temple and Jacob's Ladder. The normal representation of the Deity in Craft symbolism is the letter G. The arms of the Antient (Ancient) Grand Lodge include the Man, the Eagle, the Lion and the Bull. All these are derived from Ezekiel and are figures, in turn, linked to the mystical tradition in Judaism. The three great lights in Masonry are the Volume of Sacred Law, the Square and the Compasses.

In the 18th century a major contribution was made by James Anderson, and from this point onwards the concept of' modern Freemasonry was Deist. However, it should be noted that, as with the Orange Institution in its earliest days, 'the older Masonic Operative lodges did not immediately adopt the changes of what is called Speculative Masonry' (see D Knoop and G P Junes, *The Genesis of Freemasonry* (1947) for a fuller discussion of this aspect). In his article *The Change from Christianity to Deism in Freemasonry*, J R Clarke points out that 'Christianity still had a role to play in the working of the Craft' (*Ars Quatuor) Coronatorum* 78 1965, pp 49-73). An additional factor which emphasises this point was the rapid increase in the use of the Royal Arch degree with its Christian and ancient Masonic connections (see *Gould History of Freemasonry*, Volume IV Chapters 1, 5 and 14.)

During the 18th and 19th centuries Freemasonry in Ireland and Scotland included the following degrees and rituals. In the Old Stirling Lodge in 1745 there are references to 'excellent and super excellent, five shillings', and 'Knights of Malta, five shillings'. The same lodge possesses the Stirling 'Brasses ', probably dated around the mid 1750s, which are engraved 'Knights of Malta' and 'Knight Templar'. In 1778 lodges in Scoon and Perth were conferring the degrees of Arch and Royal Mason and Knight of Malta. In October 1779 the Earl of Eglintoune, Grand Master of Lodge Mother Kilwinning, issued a chapter for a lodge in Dublin under the name High Knight Templars of Ireland Lodge. However, the practice of these so called 'high degrees' became so widespread in the Craft lodges in the period from 1750 onwards that the Grand Lodge in Scotland issued a directive in October 1880 'prohibiting and discharging its daughters to hold any meetings above the degree of Master Mason under penalty of forfeiture of their Charter' (see the official website of the Order of the Temple, The Great Priory of Scotland for a fuller discussion).

David Stevenson, in his recent book, *The Origins of Freemasonry: Scotland's Century: 1590-1710*, attempts to revise the accepted view that Freemasonry moved from Operative to Speculative at the creation of the Grand Lodge in London 1717. According to Stevenson, modern-day freemasonry emerged during the 17th century at the time of the Renaissance, not the Enlightenment. He claims that William Schaw, the Kings Master of Work, declared himself 'generall Wardene' of Scottish Masons in 1598 and 1599 (p 34), the so called 'Schaw Statutes'.

He added that he provided Scottish Masons with rituals based on hermetic thought (Hermeticism and the teachings of people such as Giordano Bruno flowed into almost all aspects of Renaissance culture). He cites Sir Robert Moray, initiated in 1641. and his choice of the pentangle as his personal symbol and Masons' mark. However, he goes on to add that there is little evidence to link Freemasonry with hermetic thought (p 49).

Within modern Freemasonry, the following degrees operate. Firstly, 'Blue' masonry, which includes Entered Apprentice, Fellow Craft and Master Mason. The first two predate 1717, while the third was formed in the early 1700s. The first two are based on rituals used by the early stonemason guilds of the early Middle Ages, with some references to features in King Solomon's Temple. The third is the enactment of a medieval legend about Hiram Abiff, the murdered architect of King Solomon's Temple. He appears in the Old Testament 1 Kings 7:13-40 as the Phoenician craftsman hired for the bronze work in the temple because the Israelites lacked the necessary skills. But we are also told (2 Chronicles 2:11-14), that he is the son of the daughter of the tribe of Dan and in 1 Kings 7:14, he becomes the 'widow's son' of a different tribe, that of Naphtali. So it is a little confusing!

The two bronze pillars of the Temple are significant in the Masonic degrees. Their names, Jachin - 'The Lord will establish his throne for ever' and Boaz - 'In the strength of the Lord the king will rejoice' - is a plausible interpretation as they may have been the initial words of dynastic oracles (see Peake p 342 for a fuller discussion). In the third degree he becomes the master builder in charge of the construction of the Temple. He is murdered and the search for his body and recovery form the basis of the degree. Within Freemasonry, the Hiram Abiff story is widely interpreted in the context of a Euhemerism belief system with the emphasis that myth and legend are the consequences of historical events. As the origins of Freemasonry are lost in time, only the allegory survived and this was accepted as factual. Hiram Abiff became a real person and it was taught that the order was founded by the workmen who built the Temple. In 11 Chronicles, Solomon sends to Huram, King of Tyre for help in building the Temple (in the Book of Kings Huram is called Hiram). Huram sends Hiram a son of the daughter of the tribe of Dan (11 Chronicles 2: Verses 11-14). However in 1 Kings 7:14 he is called the widows son of the tribe of Naphati. Out of this combination emerges Hiram Abiff (the latter word is a corruption from the Hebrew and it can be translated as 'my master'. However, most modern day Masons now accept that the story is a legend.

The Hiram legend did not always form such a central role. In the Masonic document, the Graham Manuscript, dated 24 October 1726, one finds references to the sons of Noah seeking a secret which their dead father had possessed, in a ritual similar to that of the modern day third degree. The three sons, Shem, Ham and Japheth, go to a grave and attempt to raise the body. In trying to lift him up they pull on a finger, which comes away. They then attempt to raise the body by pulling it by the wrist and elbow .This is unsuccessful and they eventually raise the body by way of a five-point hold (see www.royalarch.org/mmmh003, Noah and Freemasonry).

A major figure in the shifting of the emphasis to Hiram Abiff would appear to be the Rev Jean Theophilus Desaguliers, Grand Master of the Grand Lodge of England, 1719-1722. He was French, educated at Corpus Christi College Oxford and later a Fellow of the Royal Society. In 1730 a more detailed account of the death of

Hiram Abiff was published. (See *Freemasonry Today*, winter 2000/2001 Issue 15, *Following in Noah's Footsteps*, for a fuller discussion.)

The other Masonic degrees are normally referred to as Red. The degree of Royal Arch, probably of French origin, is one. In the early period it was linked to the Antient group. Within British Masonry there are two different themes in the rituals, both stemming from the story of Solomon's Temple. In England it is considered to be the completion of the third degree, with the loss of the Master Mason's word being found in the Royal Arch. Some Masonic groupings call this the Tetragrammaton, a term used outside Judaism for the holiest name of God, YHVH. From the Greek for four letters.

In masonry the password of a Master Mason was lost when Hiram Abiff was murdered. According to legend, King Solomon established a new word, nowadays called the 'Master Mason's Word'. However, in the Scottish Rite more than one word exists, depending on which degree the candidate has reached (I shall return to the Scottish Rite later in this analysis). In answer to the charge that the Craft degrees were rewritten to create the Royal Arch degree, Bernard E Jones says that there is no evidence to support this statement (p 576).

A minute book from 1752 is the oldest Irish reference to the Royal Arch Chapter degree. (see K B Jackson, Beyond the Craft, pp 9-10). In his history of the Royal Arch degree in Ireland James Penny (RAC No 253) says that the Royal Arch Chapter was well established by 1754. He refers to the transactions of the Irish Lodge of Research No. 200, 1923, which show that in 1730 the Hiramic legend and the Royal Arch degree were worked as well as a separate

Chair degree. He refers to a ceremony, now elaborated into the Installed Master's degree, the Royal Arch and the Red Cross Mason, known in Scotland and England as the Red Cross of Babylon or the Red Cross Knight or Babylon Pass.

In the early part of the 19th century the Irish degrees were grouped into the following (1) Entered Apprentice, Fellow Craft and Master Mason: (2) Past Master Excellent Mason, Super Excellent Mason, Arch Mason, Royal Arch Mason: (3) Ark Mason, Mark Fellow Mason, Mark Mason, Link Mason or Wrestle, Babylonian Pass or Red Cross of Daniel, Jordan Pass, Royal Order or Prussian Blue and (4) High Knight Templar etc.

The degrees of 'Excellent' and 'Super Excellent' are now part of the veil ceremony in the Royal Arch. Penny adds that some of the other degrees are now in use, but others have found their way into the Black Institution. In 1805 the Grand Lodge of Ireland tried to exercise more control over the Craft lodges working the higher degrees by introducing a system of Warrants, but this was unpopular. The Royal Arch degree was worked in Craft lodges up to 1856. Today the Mark Master Mason degree is the precursor to the Royal Arch .

In Ireland the ritual of the Royal Arch deals with the repair of the Temple under Josiah, circa 650 BC, and thus is truer to the biblical text (2 Chronicles Chapter 34, Verses 1-14). This point is emphasised by W A Moore in his discussion of the Irish Royal Arch legend, when he points out that it differs from the American York Rite, the Scottish Rite and the English Royal Arch in that the principal characters are King Josiah, Shaphan and Hilkiah the Priest (pp 19-27). However, in Scotland and England the ceremonies include the re-enactment of the discovery of a vault amid the destruction of the Temple where there lies hidden a scroll and an altar, a legend which may originate from the Apocrypha. The Second Book of Maccabees tells the story of Jeremiah hiding the tabernacle, the Ark and the Altar of Incense in a hollow cave. The Irish masons wear their aprons under their jackets, as the repair took place at a time when Israel was at peace.

Other bodies worked the degree at a time some 100 years later, when the Jewish people had received their freedom from Cyrus, the King of Persia, and returned to Jerusalem to rebuild the Temple under Zerubbabel (Ezra Chapter 5: Verses 1-6), a period in Jewish history, worked in Ireland under the Grand Council of Knight Masons. In Ireland there are two side degrees above the Royal Arch, the Grand Council of Knight Masons and the Great Priory of Ireland.

As with many of the degrees above Master Mason, some Masonic jurisdictions place the Royal Arch within a separate organisation. (Note that a similar situation exists with the Royal Arch Purple Order and the Orange Order in a different context.) Also, different versions of the Royal Arch degree exist. Within the Scottish Rite it is placed in the time of Solomon but long after Hiram Abiff has died. In others it is set in the time of the Babylonian Captivity. The traditional colour is Red and its emblem is the Triple Tau. Within this degree the Triple Tau has the following meanings, which the ritual gives in Latin and English:

Temple Hierosolyma - the Temple of Jerusalem
Clavis ad Thesaurum - a key to a treasure
Theca ubi res pretiosa deponitur - a place where a precious
thing is concealed
Res ipsa pretiosa - the precious thing itself

(See The Hiram Key pp 414-419 for an interesting discussion on this aspect.)

In Britain it is restricted to Christians, with limited access to the degree and refers to itself as the Ancient and Accepted Rite. (On a letter heading in my possession, for the Knights of Malta No 7 Sentinel Royal Black Encampment, Belfast, 188?, the Triple Tau within a six-pointed cross with the slogan Pro Deo Et Patria (For God and Country) appears).

The so called Scottish degrees are most probably of Jacobite French origin and the major figure was a Chevalier Ramsay, with his claim that masonry had its origins in the knightly orders of the Crusades. It is very likely that the notion that these degrees had possibly Jacobite French origins, with a perceived links to the Roman Catholic Church, would have been unacceptable to many of the Protestants in Ireland. Perhaps this is yet another reason for the rejection of the link to Scotland and the 'higher degrees' by some Protestants, such as Rogers.

The predecessor for the Ancient and Accepted Scottish Rite was the Order of the Royal Secret. This consisted of 25 degrees. Within the tradition of Freemasonry the lodges of this Rite came to America via Bordeaux. The name Ancient and Accepted Scottish Rite first appeared in an 1804 agreement between the Supreme Council of France and the Grand Orient of France. Thus, despite its name, it has no Scottish origins. As a matter of fact it was not until 1846 that a Supreme Council was set up in Scotland. In America it has two jurisdictions, Northern and Southern. Under the influence of Albert Pike it spread beyond America into Europe, South America and the Southern Hemisphere.

In the Southern Jurisdiction the following degrees operate:

The Lodge of Perfection (the following degrees are linked to the Ineffable Name of God and moral values)

4th degree Secret Master

5th degree Perfect Master

6th degree Intimate Secretary

7th degree Intendant of the Building

8th degree Provost and Judge

9th degree Elu of Nine

10th degree Elu of Fifteen

11th degree Elu of Twelve

12th degree Master Architect

13th degree Royal Arch of Solomon

14th degree Perfect Elu

Chapter of Rose Croix (reflecting matters of religion and ethics)

15th degree Knight of the Sword

16th degree Prince of Jerusalem

17th degree Knight of the East and West

18th degree Knight of Rose Croix of Heredom

Council of Kadosh (reflecting concepts of chivalry, justice and responsibility)

19th degree Grand Pontiff

20th degree Master of the Symbolic Lodge

21st degree Prussian Knight or Noachite

22nd degree Knight of the Royal Axe or Prince of Libanus

23rd degree Chief of the Tabernacle

24th degree Prince of the Tabernacle

25th degree Knight of the Brazen Serpent

26th degree Prince of Mercy or Scottish Trinitarian

27th degree Knight Commander of the Temple

28th degree Knight of the Sun or Prince Adept

29th degree Scottish Knight of St Andrew

30th degree Knight Kadosh

Consistory (relating to matters of spiritual and temporal wellbeing)

31st degree Inspector Inquisitor

32nd degree Master of the Royal Secret

Supreme Council (an Order of Merit)

33rd degree Sovereign Grand Inspector General

(see Rex R Hutchens for further details.)

According to the website of the Californian Scottish Rite the above degrees simply amplify and elaborate on the lessons of the Craft degrees, adding that there is no higher degree than that of Master Mason.

In the United Kingdom the Rite is restricted to Christians, with limited access to the degrees, and the name Scottish is dropped. It refers to itself as the Ancient and Accepted Rite.

Another major degree structure within Masonry is the York Rite. In Britain this includes the first three Craft degrees, the Past Masters and the Holy Royal Arch. In America the degrees are worked with the following Biblical readings:

Mark Master: linked to Matthew 20, 1-16; 21, 42; Mark 12,10; Luke 20,17; Acts 4,11; and Revelations 2,17 (Californian jurisdiction substitutes 2 Chronicles 2,16, Ezekiel 44 1-3. (See ritual of the Grand Chapter of Royal Arch Masons of the state of California, 1974 pp 20-21.)

Past Master, based on lessons in Psalm 25.

Most Excellent Master, which is linked to 2 Chronicles 6-7 and 1 Kings 7-8.

Royal Arch: refers to the lessons taught in 2 Chronicles Chapter 36. The ceremonies are based upon the return of Israelites from captivity to build a destroyed temple.

This is under the jurisdiction of Cryptic Masonry, a term thought to refer to the legend of a crypt beneath Solomon's Temple which contained secrets.

Royal Master (1 Kings 5-7); Select Master (Deuteronomy 31, 24-26), considered by some to be the summit and perfection of Antient masonry.

Super Excellent Master: the main function would appear to be the wisdom of worshipping God. The degree is dedicated to Aaron the High Priest and to those appointed by King Solomon.

Under the jurisdiction of Commanderies of Knight Templar:

Illustrious Order of the Red Cross (Ezra 3, 4 and 6).

Mediterranean Pass and Order of Malta (based on the times of the Crusades and the first is a necessary precondition for a safe pilgrimage and journey to the Holy Sepulchre and it ends with enrolment into the Order of Malta.

The Order of the Temple (which links Christian virtues with promise of immortality and the Word becoming flesh). Other degrees with Biblical references include:

The Order of High Priesthood (Genesis 14:1-3:8:24 and 33:18-20).

Order of the Silver Trowel (1 Kings 1:5-34: Psalm 19, the closing years of King David's life).

Order of the Red Cross of Constantine (with references to Constantine the Great after the battle of Saxa Ruba 312 A.D).

Order of Knight Masons (Ezra 3, 4 and 5), whose members control the Green degrees of Ireland. These were founded in Ireland around 1923 for the purpose of governing the degrees formally controlled by the Order of Knight Templars in Ireland. The degrees are Knight of the Sword, Knight of the East, Knight of the East and the West and Installed Excellent Chief. Members are required to be Royal Arch Masons.

Clearly, many of the 'higher' degrees have references to stories in the Old and the New Testament. It is therefore possible that some of the degrees at present found in the Royal Black Institution and the Knight s of Malta had their origins within Masonry and, when they were incorporated into these organisations, modifications took place to alter the structure from the original sources. It would seem to be a reasonable assumption that in the 18th century, many fraternal organisations used structures and terminology redolent of Masonry. However, imitation does not necessarily equal similarity. For example, as I have indicated earlier, within the umbrella structure of the Orange Institution, but separately, there is the Royal Arch Purple Order, a separate degree. The structure and working of it are based on the Holy Bible and the prayers are Christian. Thus although the title is similar to the Masonic Royal Arch degree, that is where it starts and ends. The Irish version of the former is based on the theme of the Exodus to the Promised Land. Broadly speaking, the Masonic Craft degrees are linked to the construction of Solomon's Temple and the Royal Arch degree relates to its rebuilding.

At the conferring of the Royal Arch Purple degree, the following biblical readings are used. (See HRAPO p 194 ff for a fuller discussion).

Exodus Chapter 13 v 15-18

Numbers Chapter 14v 11, 12, 26-28, 33.

Joshua Chapter 5 v 13-15

Psalm 107: 4-8, 12-15

Psalm 106: 43-45

Genesis Chapter 28: 10-14

1 Corinthians Chapter 13, v 13

1 Corinthians Chapter 15 vv 56, 57

Genesis Chapter 1 vv 14-18

John Chapter 1 v 5

Exodus Chapter 13 vv 21, 22

1 Corinthians Chapter 15 v 58

Revelations Chapter 22 v 21

In the Masonic Royal Arch degrees the following readings are to be found:

Proverbs Chapter 2

Exodus 3, V, 1-6:13, 14

Exodus Chapter 4 v 1-5:6-9

II Chronicles 35 v 11-20 (in America it is 2 Chronicles 36)

Exodus 6 v2-3.

Proverbs 2:1-9 and 3:13-20.

Haggai 2:1-9

II Kings 22:3-13

II Chronicles 34:8-21

1 John Chapter v 1-5.

Clearly, within Freemasonry, there are degrees which include references to situations or developments in the Old and the New Testament. Also, above the entrance of many Masonic Halls the phrase 'Fiat Lux' (Let there be light) is clearly written. This is a reference to the first act of God's creation of the World (Genesis 1.3). However, within this organisation there are also references to the Great Architect of the Universe – a Deist concept, which allows the Christian Holy Bible to be substituted for the Holy books of other faiths. However, as I have earlier pointed out, certain degrees are open only to Christians. So could there be a Masonic connection with the degrees structures of the Royal Black Institution and the Knights of Malta?

CHAPTER SIX

THE DEGREE STRUCTURE OF THE ROYAL BLACK INSTITUTION, THE KNIGHTS OF MALTA AND FREEMASONRY

In order to carry out this examination it is necessary to outline the present degree structure of these orders. It is to be regretted that RBI and the Knights of Malta are not as open as Masonry in this respect. Accordingly the following is partly drawn from their official publications and partly from personal information. As the latter were obtained in situations linked to secrecy the references will, by their nature, be oblique and perhaps only fully understood by members of the orders. Furthermore, it has to be remembered that this study is not an exposé of either organisation. Where appropriate I will indicate possible links to degrees within Masonry. Firstly the degrees of the Royal Black Institution:

Black degree
Scarlet degree
Mark degree (overlaps with Super Excellent Master and Royal Master in Masonry)
Apron degree (overlaps with the third degree in Masonry)
Royal Blue degree (overlaps with Royal Arch and the third degree in Masonry)

71

White degree

Royal Green (overlaps with Ark Mariner degree in Masonry)

Gold degree

Star and Garter degree (overlaps with Super Excellent Master in Masonry).

Crimson Arrow degree

Link and Chain degree

Red Cross degree (a degree with a similar title exists in Masonry and a fuller discussion will follow)

The Order of the Knights of Malta.

An examination of the minute books of Knights of Malta encampments working in the 19th century shows that the working degrees had the following titles: Knight of Malta, Royal Black, Royal Scarlet, Royal Mark , Blue or Supreme Architect or Blue Man Master Builder, White or Knight of Israel, Gold, Green, Priestly Pass, Red Cross or Pale Red Cross, Great Cross Degree of Merit.

Today the Order operate the following degree structure:

Knight Hospitaller degree

Knight of Malta degree. This title is found in a degree in Masonry. (This degree will be outlined more fully later in this chapter).

Scarlet degree

Mark degree (overlaps with Super Excellent Master and the third degree in Masonry).

Blue degree (overlaps with same references as above degree).

White degree.

Green degree (overlaps with Ark Mariner degree in Masonry).

Gold degree

Priestly Pass degree (overlaps with Super Excellent Master degree in Masonry).

Master Builder degree (overlaps with the Third degree in Masonry).

Apron degree

Red Cross degree (a degree with a similar title exists in Masonry and a fuller outline will follow).

Great Cross degree (an Order of Merit which originated in the USA).

In the Annual Report of the Imperial Parent Encampment 1933, there is a reference to reviving the Degree of Royal Sovereign Master to replace the Great Cross Degree. However I can find no further indications as to the working of this degree.

In the Malta Bulletin dated May 1971, the following descriptions of the American versions of these degrees are given. First it is pointed out that every Sir Knight wears a red plume in his hat, shoulder straps and a baldric, whether an officer or not.

The twelve degrees are as follows:

Knight of Malta

Royal Scarlet (derived from the Orange institution)

Royal Black

Royal Mark (Masonic derivation)

Royal Blueman Master Builder (Masonic derivation)

Royal Gold (Orange derivation)

Royal Green

Royal White

Knight of the Green

Priestly Pass (the old order of priesthood or chaplain)

Red Cross (traditionally founded by the Emperor Constantine).

Other editions refer to a Past Commanders degree and Red Cross and Sepulchre degree. Many editions refer to the College of Ancients and the working of a Sublime degree. In an edition of the *Daily News* dated April 8 1908, an article refers to the Knights of Malta of Beaver Falls 'conferring the Order of the Red Cross and the Sepulchre, the 12th degree of the Order at their hall in the Benson Building'.

Although the degree structure and rituals of the RBI and the Knights of Malta do have some elements in common, they are separate and are not interchangeable. However, it would be possible to claim that the younger order did draw from the older in the early days of the formation of the RBI when some of the original degrees were altered. Also, some of the material in the degrees in both orders clearly drew from those of Masonry (see earlier references to the work of James Penny in relation to the RBI and the symbolism found on the letterhead for Sentinel No 7 Encampment). In particular note the parts of the degrees that deal with the construction and discovery of the various Temples referred to in the Old and New Testament.

These in turn are linked to the changing concept of the notion of God in scripture and in the rituals. For example, the Old Testament (OT) refers to Him as walking in the Garden of Eden in the cool of the day (Genesis Chapter 3:8). Also He is said to have repented that man was made on Earth and to be grieved (Genesis Chapter 6:6: Chapter 11:5-7, 18 Chapter 32:24-32).

The earliest names are El, the name of the chief god in the Ugaritic pantheon and Elohim, which generally refer to a power above humans. El-Shadda (i) – God Almighty - is the name by which He is known to the patriarchs (Genesis Chapter 17:1, 28:3, 35:11, 48:3, 49:25, Exodus Chapter 6:3).

After the Exile the Jews ceased to pronounce the

Tetragrammaton, YHWH, for reasons of homage linked to Exodus 20:7 and Leviticus 24:16.Thus the sacred name was substituted by Adonai or Lord. The name is revealed to Moses just before the Exodus (Chapter 6:3) and it was the Covenant or Personal Name by which God becomes known to the Chosen People. Later the name Jehovah is used, which is based on the consonants JHVH or JIIVH, because in Hebrew the consonants are formally written and the vowels were supplied by the reader, so the true pronunciation is lost.

However, as the degree rituals move into the area of the New Testament (NT) God takes on the role of Father of the individual not the Father of Israel (Matthew Chapter 6:9. 26:32, 7:9-11 and 10:29-31). Furthermore everyone is a son of God in Christ (Romans Chapter 8:15-17, Galatians 4:6, Peter 1:6, Matthew 5:45. In Luke Chapter 6:35 God becomes the Father of all Mankind.

The rituals of the degrees also reflect a change in the meaning and significance of the term temple as they move from the OT to the NT references. This enables one to tackle the question as to why the rituals of Christian orders of Knighthood refer to the manual building of a temple when in Christian thinking the notion of a physical temple is rejected for a bodily temple.

The first reference in the OT to a temple is to be found in Exodus Chapter 24:4, when Moses builds a type of temple containing an altar ringed by 12 pillars. This structure need not concern us, as the important ritually-based Temple is that of Solomon. His Temple is built after the model of the Tabernacle – the inner tent available for worship. The furniture was similar, but not identical. Under him it became the dwelling place of Yahweh: 'I have surely built thee a house to dwell in, a settled place for thee to abide in for ever' (1 Kings Chapter 8:13, the words used by

Solomon to dedicate the Temple). The planning and building details are outlined in 2 Samuel, 1 Kings and 1 Chronicles. In 1 Kings we are told that the Assyrians capture Jerusalem and destroy the Temple and the population are driven into exile (Psalms 137:1).

Later the Persian King Cyrus allows the Jews to return from captivity and in 558 BCE (Before the Christian Era) orders that the House of Yahweh 'in Jerusalem, which is in Judah' be rebuilt (1 Chronicles Chapter 36:23: Ezra Chapter 1:2-4). A Persian official, a Babylonian Jew, Sheshbazzar, helps to lay the foundations, but the work is stopped (Ezra Chapter 6:3-5).

At this stage of the history of the Temple a puzzling feature emerges in the story. The author of Chronicles would appear to have rewritten the story of the finding of the Book of the Law in the first Temple when it was rebuild by King Josiah. In 2 Kings Chapter 22:8 the scroll that is 'discovered' is called the Book of the Law in the House of the Lord, but in 2 Chronicles Chapter 34:14 it is referred to as the Book of the Law given through Moses (these are the readings found in the working of the Irish Royal Arch Masonic degree).

The Second Temple, also referred to as the Temple of Zerubbabel, is built in the same place as that of Solomon's. Its principal parts are a reproduction, but the Jews felt it was inferior to that of Solomon's because it was missing five key features:

(1) The Ark of the Covenant

(2) The Shechinah or manifestation of the Lord as referred to in Exodus Chapter 24:16:1 Kings Chapter 8 as a cloud of brightness, and borrowed by Christianity in the NT Matthew Chapter 17:5, Luke Chapter 2:9 and Acts Chapter 7:55.

(3) The Urim and the Thummim – the Light and Perfection by which the High Priest enquired of the Lord (Exodus Chapter 28:30, Leviticus Chapter 8:8, Numbers Chapter 27:21, Deuteronomy Chapter 33, Isaiah Chapter 28:6). It has been suggested that they are either stones in the High Priest's breastplate, sacred dice or little images of truth and justice. They do not exist after the Captivity (Ezra Chapter 2:63).

(4) The Holy Fire upon the altar

(5) The Spirit of Prophecy.

This temple stood for some 500 years until it was replaced by Herod in 19 BCE in an attempt to win popularity with the Jews. It was later destroyed (Mark Chapter 13.1, 2). It is possible that the rebuilding of the Temple is also linked to a growth in the sense of a Jewish identity which focused on the Temple. For example the Essenes and in particular the settlement at Qumran held a vision to rebuild it with a new priesthood. They believed that the Temple and its rites were a corruption and illegitimate. The image was based on Ezekiel's and Solomon's Temple but with features linked back to the Tabernacle in the desert period. However, perhaps to encourage the Jews of the period to retain a vision of a better future, the author of the Second Book of Baruch states that the destroyed earthly Temple will be preserved in heaven.

The Book of Ezekiel opens and closes with a vision of the Glory of God. He describes another temple, which never existed. Ezekiel has a vision that Israel was restored to its former status and that Solomon's Temple had arisen from the ruins. This is most likely to be a lesson in morality to Israel along the lines of a heavenly design (Ezekiel Chapters 40-48). These references are also found in the ritual of the Masonic Mark Master degree, although in an abbreviated form.

In the NT the Temple is absent. The Christian scriptures refer to a Temple that could not be built on Earth. In the three Synoptic Gospels the writers are aware of the destruction of the Jerusalem Temple as Jesus predicts it (Matthew Chapter 24:2: Mark Chapter 13:2 and Luke Chapter 21:6).

So what we now have is a temple religion without a physical temple. In its place we have the concept of the Lamb of God. In the Old Testament references are made to lambs used as a means of atonement for sins, eg Leviticus 4:32-34, 16:21 and 5:6. The blood of the sacrificial lamb is smeared on the doorposts and lintels of each household during the Passover (Exodus 12:1-28). Lambs are sacrificed in the Temple for the sins of the people (Exodus 29:38-42). In Jeremiah 11:19 and Isaiah 53:7 references are made to the coming of 'One who will be like a Lamb to the slaughter' and whose sacrifice would provide redemption for Israel. However Christians refer to Jesus as the Lamb of God and the ultimate sacrifice for sin in John 1:29 and 1:36, Romans 8:3. In revelations 14:1 the Messiah is represented by a lamb. Many Jewish scholars reject this Christian interpretation of Isaiah 52:7. They claim that the term 'Lamb of God' does not refer to a sacrificial animal, pointing out that in Galilean Aramaic the word 'talya' (lamb) can refer to a male child. (See Vermes, 2001, for a fuller discussion and analysis of this issue.)

In John Chapter 2:16 Jesus speaks of the destruction of the Temple in words Christians inferred as meaning his own death and resurrection. He in effect becomes the everlasting Temple. The most important reference is to be found in John: 'Destroy the

Temple and in three days I will raise it up again'. This was interpreted by his followers to mean that his resurrection would bring forth a new Temple - Jesus himself - and through Him the presence of God would be felt. It was Paul who developed this into a greater comprehension of the changing concept of the Temple to Christians and from his writings and sayings emerge the notion of a bodily temple.

In the later history of the church, figures such as St Jerome return to the notion of a destroyed temple as an example of the punishment of the Jews. However, one has only to look to later church architecture and in particular the creation of the cathedrals to note that a physical temple is created on Earth.

It would appear that not all sections of Christianity were comfortable with the links between the portrayal of Jesus and the Lamb of God. For example, in 692 CE Justinian summoned a Council to review ecclesiastical law. It legislated for the first time on religious art and it prescribes, in Canon 82, the image of the Saviour in his human form, rather than the earlier symbol of the Lamb of God. (see *Byzantium* by Judith Herrin, p 95-7, for a fuller discussion on this point).

Thus the paradox; on the one hand, the issue of a destroyed temple as a defeat of Judaism and the rise of Christianity and on the other, the image of a Temple as a reflection of a spirituality pervading Christianity. We find that the rituals and degrees of these Christian orders reflect this tension and hence their movement in and out of OT and NT readings and references with the appropriate imagery displayed in the symbols of the orders. This in turn forms a link between the Patriarchal Era and the Christian Era.

This paradox is also to be found in the working of the Royal

Arch Purple Order degree, with its overlapping references to the OT and the NT. The story of the Children of Israel and the symbolism of Jesus Christ is linked to the notions of forgiveness and redemption.

To return to the degrees in both orders entitled Red Cross and their possible link to Masonry. In the Masonic degree called the Masonic and Military order of the Red Cross of Constantine, the jewel carries the inscription IHSV. This degree and its ritual belong to what are termed the 'East and West' rites. In effect it consists of three degrees - Knight, Priest Mason and Prince Mason. The first stage of the initiation consists of the legend of Constantine the Great's conversion to Christianity. The candidate arrives as a 'Knight of Rome' who wishes to embrace Christianity. (For a fuller discussion and explanation of the other two stages, see the website of the Cumbrian Masons.) Linked to this order are the Knight of the Holy Sepulchre and the Knight of St John the Evangelist. The latter gives a Christian vision of the Royal Arch ceremony and the former has no connection with the mediaeval order of the same name. The legend suggests that the pagan Constantine had a vision of a shining cross of light which bore the inscription 'Conquer with this' or 'By this sign you will conquer' (Hoc Signo Victor Eris). That night all is explained to him in a dream and he is ordered to make a replica of the sign and to use it as a protection against his enemies. The effect of the symbol and the manner in which his enemies viewed it implanted in Constantine the belief that he had to follow the Christian God.

After the victory at Milvian Bridge in 312 he declined to thank the pagan gods at the Altar of Victory. Eusebuis, the Bishop of Caesavea circa 313-340, records his adherence to Christianity and other historians emphasize his worship of Sol Invictus. Whether or not the vision is a myth he nevertheless spent most of his later life as a patron of Christianity. He was buried as a Christian in a mausoleum along with relics of the 12 Apostles. (For a fuller discussion see *The Emperor Constantine*, Michael Grant 1998 and *Eusebius: Life of Constantine*.)

A prominent and distinguishing symbol in the RBI is that of a Red Cross set within a Crown. Within the Knights of Malta the distinguishing symbol is that of an eight-pointed White Maltese Cross and within it a Red Cross with the letters IHSV denoting 'in this (sign) you will conquer' a rendition in Latin from the Greek. This also appears in the Knight Templar Cross of the York Rite. One can also find the symbol of the Maltese Cross and the Red Cross surmounted by IHGMYBA in the older images of the Knights of Malta.

On the website of the Columbus York Rite (USA) the following Orders of Knighthood are conferred by Columbus Commandery No 39 Knights Templar.

The Illustrious Order of the Red Cross

This consists of two sections. The first depicts Zerubbabel's admission to the Jewish Council at Jerusalem, in which he receives permission and authority to travel to Babylon and attempts to stop the enemies of the Jews from hindering the building of the temple and to recover the holy vessels of the temple. The second section takes place in the court of Darius, where Zerubbabel is granted a position in the royal household.

The Order of Malta

This is a combination of the Order of St Paul (Mediterranean Pass) and the Order of Malta. The former is based on St Paul's shipwreck on the island of Melita (Malta). The candidate is a knight who about to depart for the Crusades. The latter presents the history of the Order and a discussion of the life, death and resurrection of Jesus Christ. It is a preparation for the next degree, in that the candidate receives additional instruction in the New Testament, particularly the eight Beatitudes.

The Order of the Temple

The candidate enters as a Knight of Malta who wishes to join a Commandery of Knights Templar. To test his faith he is required to go on a pilgrimage, then to undertake a period of warfare. Having performed these activities he is admitted. He is then required to undertake a period of penance before becoming a Knight Templar.

CHAPTER SEVEN

CONCLUSIONS

The organisations I have examined in this book are societies with secrets. In other words, their rituals and symbolism are only fully understood by those who are initiated members. These rituals and symbols are, in turn, a method of teaching historical connections between the Old Testament and the New Testament, the development of the changing concept and role of God in the universe, a framework for the proper way to lead one's life, and a morality tale. They are not subversive or anti-democratic movements with political aims. If anything they should be viewed as a form of social activity. Thus in form and structure they are very much the product of the fraternal societies of the early 16th and 17th centuries.

The rise of the Orange Order and the development of its degree structure should be seen in the context of a period of political unrest, hence the creation of passwords and signs as a means of identifying friend from foe. At that time lodges of Freemasons were a feature of social life in this part of Ireland. Some of the founders of the Orange Order were actively involved in Masonic lodges and as a consequence the use of passwords, rituals and initiation ceremonies would be familiar to them.

At the time of the formation of the Knights of St John, the Knights of Malta, their official historian, Gilmour, claims that the patron saint was St John the Almoner. This is disputed by Sire, who says that the hospice was dedicated to St John the Baptist with a lay membership under Augustine Rule. However, another writer, MacLennon, disagrees. He claims the Order was Benedictine and only later did it come under the Augustine Rule. The present day Protestant Knights of Malta conform to Gilmour's claim.

Over the next century or so the Order became organised into seven and later eight languages. The divisions within Christianity that resulted in and from the Reformation affected the Order. By the end of the 17th century Napoleon had expelled them from Malta and in 1834 the Roman Catholic section had found a home in Rome.

In relation to the Order in Scotland, the information is confusing and conflicting. Sire notes that the Order obtained its first possessions from King David I at Torphichen, perhaps around 1124, whereas Rembower and Gray claim that a distinctly Scottish branch emerged in 1163 with David I as the Grand Prior or Master. According to Sire, by 1199 the Order had 28 active preceptories in England.

In Ireland the Order was well established under the tutelage of Strongbow and by 1212 some 29 preceptories were actively working. In 1540, Henry VIII imposed his control over them. However, the English Language Branch retained Torphichen and in 1564 Sir James Sandilands surrendered it to the Crown and in return received the title of Lord Torphichen.

In their study, Cowan, Mackay and Macquarrie find that the earliest reference to the Order in Scotland is 1434 and that during the next century or so William Knollis obtained a grant of the preceptory until 1510. After this date the grant moved to George Dundas, who was succeeded by Walter Lindsay, who in turn was succeeded by Sandilands of Calder. In February 1563 or 1564 he gave all the property to the Crown and according to Cowan et al the Order ceased to exist in Scotland from that date.

Not so, according to Gilmour. He claims that as the writ of Henry VIII did not apply to Scotland, which was Protestant, the Order was not suppressed. Central to this claim was the role played by the Protestant Sir James Sandilands and his adherence to the teaching of John Knox. Rembower and Gray also claim that Protestant Knights existed in Scotland and England in 1557. Furthermore, they claim that by 1643 the Order was reintroduced into Ireland to protect Protestants and that this Branch still existed in 1795 when the Orange and Black were linked.

These latter claims are linked to the findings of a report of the Knights of Malta dated 11 April 1850, Dublin, part of which describes the history of the Order in Scotland. In this report the validity of the Grand Black Chapter of Ireland – the RBI - is challenged . Gilmour cites evidence dating back to 1795 which separates the Order from the Orange Order. Documents dated 1814, 1816, 1821 and 1829 are used to show that the Knights of Malta existed prior to 1831 and are thus the older of the Black Orders of Knighthood.

In the late 19th century and in periods of the 20th century many organisations laid claim to the original Order of the Knights of Malta. Upon examining the claims of these orders I have reached the conclusion that they have no links with the original Knights of Malta.

The background to the emergence of the RBI and its effects are dealt with in Chapter 5. I have attempted to emphasize that the chaotic state of affairs in Ireland resulted in the links with Scotland being difficult to maintain. The issue over the Higher degrees in the Orange Order, the selling of warrants and the holding of illegal meetings all led to the relative decline in status and influence of the Knights of Malta. Nevertheless, Gilmour cites a series of connections with the Orange Order and the Knights of Malta. For example, in 1861 and 1867 warrants of the latter Order were still being given by the Scottish section to Ireland.

This episode is taken up by Aiken McClelland, who in a series of publications dealing with the formation of the RBI he comments on the hostility of the leaders of the Orange Order to the issue of the so called 'Higher Degrees'. They were perceived as a challenge to the legal status of the Orange Order, and furthermore some of the degrees clearly annoyed the leadership of the Order, which was composed of the gentry and the professional class of Dublin. This situation was resolved when the RBI became a separate organisation in or around 1863.

The contribution of Edward Rogers, the first Grand Registrar of the RBI, is central to this debate. His accounts of events are in conflict with both those of Gilmour and McClelland and I would suggest that readers reach their own conclusions as to which side was the more historically accurate. Rogers goes on to attack the creation of the Grand Britannic Institution and the Grand Council of the Knights of Malta in England and their conferring of what he terms 'Popish' degrees. Gilmour refers to the Britannic Association, presumably the same organisation, when he deals with the use of illegal warrants in Liverpool and the fluctuating fortunes of the

Order up to and around 1895. The Britannic Society or Association clearly existed in the 19th century in England and its connection to Orangeism is referred to in evidence by the Rev James Harris and M Chatwoode in their evidence to the Royal Commission in 1835.

In relation to the whole issue of the Higher Degrees I suggest that the dislike of the leaders of the Orange Institution is based on the following factors. Those who supported the working of these degrees were mainly drawn from a different social class grouping – the artisan and the merchant class. This social group was radical in its thinking and, in the main, its members were excluded from entry into Trinity College Dublin, the bastion of the Establishment. Thus they were forced to go to Scottish universities for their education. In the Scottish universities the ideals of the Enlightenment were widely discussed. Within this group the right to hold one's own opinion and make independent decisions was zealously guarded. This in turn put them in conflict with the leaders of the Orange Order over the issue of the Higher Degrees.

Within the RBI there is a strong claim that up to around 1835 the Higher or Black degrees had been mainly based on Biblical themes, but that after this date other degrees, possibly linked to Freemasonry, had been introduced. If this was so, then the supposed link to Freemasonry posed a political problem for the Protestant Order of Black Knights. Many of the founders and members of the United Irishmen were Freemasons. This factor eventually forced the leadership of Freemasonry to issue a prohibition on the discussion, within the lodge rooms, of political and religious issues. Against such a background the question of the link would have been viewed with disquiet, if not hostility, by the Protestant Orange leadership and this may well have been a factor in the resistance to the implementation of the Higher degrees.

The claim that after 1835 the 'new' degrees had non-biblical roots based on Freemasonry requires some analysis. As I have earlier noted the titles of some of the degrees in Freemasonry, the Knights of Malta and the Royal Black Institution are similar and this could well suggest a common origin. All three Orders have degree references, in one form or another, to the Temple of King Solomon. In turn some of the degree references are linked to the changing concept of God in the Old Testament and the New Testament - the Patriarchal and the Christian Eras. The degrees also reflect the changes in the meaning and significance of the use of the term Temple in both historical eras. This, in turn, allows one to explain why the rituals of the Christian Orders of Black Knighthood refer to the manual building of the Temple and the Christian notion of a spiritual Temple, not of this world, in the same breath.

The publication of the following lectures has been granted with the permission of the curator Dave Lettelier, PM, The Phoenixmasonry Masonic Museum at http://phoenixmasonry.org.

APPENDIX 1

Lecture 1 Knight of Malta

Senior Warden: Sir Knight, what were you?

Junior Warden: A novice.

Senior Warden: What then?

Junior Warden: A Knight Hospitaller.

Senior Warden: What next?

Junior Warden: A Knight of Rhodes.

Senior Warden: What are you now?

Junior Warden: A Knight of Malta.

Senior Warden: How am I to know you as such?

Junior Warden: By my being in possession of the grand countersign whereby all true Knights of Malta know and recognize each other.

Senior Warden: Will you give it to me?

Junior Warden gives grand countersign in regular form.

Senior Warden: When is it given?

Junior Warden: To the Sentinel and Warder to gain admission to the Commandery when at labour in the Knight of Malta Degree, and is the general working password of the degree.

Senior Warden: How else shall I know you?

Junior Warden: By the Pilgrim Warrior's Pass.

Senior Warden: How is it given?

Junior Warden: Under an arch of steel in a low breath only. *Wardens exemplify giving the pass.*

Sir Knight Commander: Each newly made Sir Knight will now arise and advance beneath the arch of steel and receive the Pilgrim Warrior's Pass.

All novices given pass by Commander.

Sir Knight Commander: Your attention is particularly directed to the peculiar nature of this pass and the manner and form in which it is given. This must never be forgotten as it is a vital point in your examination if visiting another Commandery. Sir Knight Wardens, you will proceed.

Senior Warden: Are you proficient in the work?

Junior Warden: I was carefully instructed and passed due examination.

Senior Warden: Give me the sword sign.

Junior Warden gives the sword sign.

Senior Warden: Give me the hailing sign.

Junior Warden gives the hailing sign; divides explanatory words with Senior Warden.

Senior Warden: Have you the grip of a Knight of Malta?

Junior Warden: Come and see. *Senior Warden gives complement.*

Senior Warden: Will you advance the test or recognition sign of a Knight of Malta?

Junior Warden: I will if you will tell me when and where it should be used.

Senior Warden: It should only be used in a duly convoked commandery, instructing a Sir Knight, or in examination of one who claims admittance.

Junior Warden gives sign. Senior Warden gives answer. Wardens salute Commander and take seats.

Choir sings 'Again Has Come the Closing Hour.'

Prelate (prayer): Almighty Father, we ask thy blessing and the outpouring of thy spirit upon all Knights of Malta and especially upon these newly-made Christian Knights. Help and guide them in the paths of truth and righteousness and may their lives be so conducted that in the end our Great Commander can say: 'Well done good and faithful servant, enter thou into the joy of thy Lord.'

All Knights: Amen. Amen. Amen.

Sir Knight Commander: The Commandery will now be at ease while we welcome these newly made Christian Knights, and after their retirement we will close in due form.

APPENDIX 2

Lecture Second Degree The Black Degree.

Senior Warden: Why do you wear that Black Robe?

Junior Warden: Because I am in mourning.

Senior Warden: For whom are you in mourning?

Junior Warden: Brother Joseph.

Senior Warden: I perceive by this you are a Companion of the Black Degree?

Junior Warden: I am always taken and accepted as such by all duly and regularly initiated Sir Knight Companions of that degree.

Senior Warden: Have you the entrance password?

Junior Warden: I have.

Senior Warden: Will you give it to me?

Junior Warden: I will if you will begin.

Senior Warden: M...

Junior Warden: S...

Senior Warden: M...

Senior Warden: What had you in your hand?

Junior Warden: A piece of money.

Senior Warden: What were you going to do with that piece of money?

Junior Warden: Purchase a piece of ground.

Senior Warden: For what purpose?

Junior Warden: To bury a brother.

Senior Warden: Where were you from?

Junior Warden: The plains of Midian.

Senior Warden: And whither were you going?

Junior Warden: To the backside of the desert, even to God's holy mount, Horeb.

Senior Warden: How did you expect to get there?

Junior Warden: By the benefit of a password.

Senior Warden: Have you that password?

Junior Warden: Who are you?

Senior Warden: I am.

Junior Warden: That I am.

Senior Warden: Pass on.

Senior Warden: When on your travels did you see anything?

Junior Warden: A great and amazing sight. A bush burning yet unconsumed.

Senior Warden: Did you hear anything?

Junior Warden: A voice saying, 'Draw not nigh hither, Moses, but cast the shoes from off thy feet, for the place whereon thou standest is holy ground,' and I did so.

Senior Warden: Have you a number?

Junior Warden: Seven.

Senior Warden: Why seven?

Junior Warden: Seven times I ascended the mountain in search of knowledge. Six times my faith failed me; but the seventh time, my faith being stronger, I gained the top and obtained it.

Senior Warden: How were you further dealt with?

Junior Warden: I was led before some throne or holy altar.

Senior Warden: What were you asked?

Junior Warden: If I could read.

Senior Warden: Could you read?

Junior Warden: No, but I paid a Prelate to read for me, who read a portion of scripture, wherein he found me guilty of all that was laid to my charge.

Senior Warden: Did Elijah command his servant to do anything?

Junior Warden: He did. To go seven times to the top of Mount Carmel, and look toward the sea. Six times he went up and saw nothing; but the seventh time he ascended he placed his hands upon his knees, and looked between his legs, and behold there was a small cloud arising out of the sea in the shape of a man's hand; and the heavens were dark with clouds, and there were signs of abundance of rain.

Senior Warden: On your advancement to this degree, how were you further dealt with?

Junior Warden: I was led a second time before some throne or holy altar.

Senior Warden: What was there demanded of you?

Junior Warden: What I stood most in need of, and I answered 'Light,' which I received at the hands of a Sir Knight Companion of this degree.

Senior Warden: On being brought to light how many lights presented themselves to your view?

Junior Warden: Twelve, representing the twelve sons of Jacob, the twelve tribes of the children of Israel, or the twelve Apostles of our Lord and Saviour Jesus Christ.

Senior Warden: What were you then commanded to do?

Junior Warden: To extinguish one of the lights and afterwards to restore it.

Senior Warden: What did the extinguished light represent?

Junior Warden: Joseph, who was sold into Egypt from amongst his brethren, or Judas Iscariot, who betrayed his Lord and Master. It also represents to me that should I ever betray any trust then or thereafter reposed in me, my light would be put out from amongst the members of this Illustrious Order.

Senior Warden: Have you the grip and mighty grand password of this degree?

Junior Warden: I have.

Senior Warden: Then, if thy heart be unto mine as mine is unto thine, stretch forth thy hand, and show thy zeal for the Lord.

Junior Warden advance grip but draw back.

Senior Warden: Why halt ye so long between two opinions? If the Lord be God, follow Him; if Baal, follow him.

Senior and Junior Warden advance grip, give it and say together: The Lord He is the God, the Lord He is the God, follow ye Him.

Senior Warden: Have you the distress sign of a Knight of Malta?

Junior Warden: I have and will give it if you will tell me when and where it should be given.

Senior Warden: It should nowhere he given except in a duly convoked Commandery, for the instruction of a Sir Knight Companion, or in case of extreme distress or danger.

Junior Warden gives distress sign.

Senior Warden: In case this sign cannot be given, what interrogatory is used?

Junior Warden: Is there no generous person here?

Senior Warden: The answer is?

Junior Warden: A friend at hand.

APPENDIX 3

Lecture Third Degree Scarlet

S.W.: Why do you wear that ribbon?

J.W.: What ribbon?

S.W.: That scarlet ribbon.

J.W.: As a true sign or token of the Scarlet degree.

S.W.: I perceive by this that you are a Scarlet Companion yourself?

J.W.: I am always taken and accepted as such by all duly and regularly initiated companions of that degree.

S.W.: How were you prepared for that degree?

J.W.: I was duly prepared by being divested of my outer garments, invested with another raiment, blindfolded, and led to the door of the Commandery.

S.W.: Where were you from?

J.W.: Shittim.

S.W.: And whither were you going?

J.W.: To spy.

S.W.: To spy what?

J.W.: To spy out secretly the whole land, even unto that great city Jericho.

S.W.: How did you expect to get there?

J.W.: By the benefit of a password.

S.W.: Have you that password?

J.W.: I have.

S.W.: Will you give it to me?

J.W.: I will if you begin.

S.W.: R...

J.W.: H...

S.W.: R... Why do you take R... for your password?

J.W.: Because she concealed the two spies.

S.W.: Where did she conceal them?

J.W.: In her house.

S.W.: Where was it situated?

J.W.: Neither in the town nor out of it.

S.W.: That must have been a curious place! Where was it ?

J.W.: Upon the town wall.

S.W.: How did she conceal them?

J.W.: With stalks of unprepared flax.

S.W.: How were they laid?

J.W.: In order.

S.W.: How in order?

J.W.: One upon two.

S.W.: Where?

J.W.: On the roof.

S.W.: Was there any covenant made between R... and those two spies?

J.W.: Have you the central password of a Scarlet Companion.

S.W.: O...

J.W.: L...

S.W.: F...

J.W.: Y...

S.W.: I...

J.W.: Y...

S.W.: U...

J.W.: N...

S.W.: T...

J.W.: O...

S.W.: B... How did those spies escape?

J. W.: Hand under hand, by means of a scarlet cord let down through the window.

S.W.: Where are they now?

J.W.: Away.

S.W.: Where to?

J.W.: The mountain.

S.W.: How long do they intend to remain there?

J.W.: Three days, or until their pursuers shall have returned from following after them.

S.W.: How was that great city of Jericho taken?

J.W.: Six days we encompassed the city round about, once each day, and on the seventh day seven times, with seven priests of the

Lord bearing seven trumpets of rams' horns before the ark of the Lord. And at 'the seventh time the priests blew with the trumpets, the people gave a great shout, the wall of the city fell down flat, every man went straight before him, and they took the city.

S.W.: Have you a number?

J.W.: I have.

S.W.: What is your number?

J.W.: Two.

S.W.: What two?

J.W.: The two spies.

S.W.: What two spies?

J.W.: The two faithful spies.

APPENDIX 4

Lecture Fourth Degree Mark

S.W.: Why do you wear that ribbon?

J.W.: What ribbon?

S.W.: That black ribbon edged with white.

J.W.: Because I both mourn and rejoice.

S.W.: Why do you both mourn and rejoice?

J.W.: Because Aaron the High Priest mourned and rejoiced.

S.W.: For whom and for what?

J.W.: He mourned for the sins of the people, and rejoiced that he had seen the glory of the Lord.

S.W.: I perceive that you are a Marksman yourself.

J.W.: I am always taken and accepted as such by all Marksmen.

S.W.: Who was the Lord's first chosen Marksman?

J.W.: Aaron.

S.W.: How was that?

J.W.: Because he wore the two breastplates whereon were engraved, within and without, the names of the twelve tribes of the Children of Israel.

S.W.: Have you the names of the two breastplates?

J.W.: I have.

S.W.: Name them.

J.W.: Urim and Thummim.

S.W.: Have you the entrance password of a Marksman?

J. W.: I have.

S.W.: Will you give it to me?

J.W.: I will if you begin.

S.W.: T...

J.W.: T...

S.W.: S... Did you ever work any?

J.W.: I did.

S.W.: Where?

J.W.: In the tower.

S.W.: Where there?

J.W.: In an inner chamber.

S.W.: Did you receive anything?

J. W.: I did.

S.W.: What did you receive?

J.W.: Wages before the work was done.

S.W.: What were those wages?

J.W.: Twelve stripes.

S.W.: Upon what did you receive them?

J.W.: My naked breech.

S.W.: How did you know there were twelve?

J.W.: Because I counted them in my hour of affliction.

S.W.: For what did you receive them?

J.W.: For disobedience of the Lord's commands.

S.W.: Did you ever travel any?

J.W.: I did.

S.W.: Where from?

J.W.: The tower to the temple.

S.W.: Why did you leave the tower and travel to the temple?

J.W.: Because the tower was confounded, but the temple was to be dedicated.

S.W.: Have you the central password of a Marksman?

J.W.: I have.

S.W.: Give it to me.

J.W.: T... T... P...

S.W.: How was the temple reared?

J.W.: Without the sound of hammer, axe, or any tool of iron. The stones were hewn in the quarry to fit, and the wood was sawed in the valley of Lebanon.

S.W.: How was it built?

J.W.: Wider above than below.

S.W.: Why?

J.W.: To signify that the heavens are wider than the earth.

S.W.: How was the temple supported?

J.W.: By three pillars.

S.W.: Name them.

J.W.: W..., S... and B...

S.W.: Why W..., S... and B...?

J.W.: W... to contrive, S... to support, and B... to adorn.

S.W.: What do Marksmen stand most in need of?

J.W.: Three great and mighty things.

S.W.: Name them.

J.W.: Faith, Hope and Truth.

S.W.: Why Faith, Hope and Truth?

J.W.: Faith to believe, Hope to be saved, and Truth to be truthful to all men, more especially to a brother Marksman, well known to be such after strict trial and due examination, or who may be vouched for by a well-known Marksman.

S.W.: Have you the great and mighty grand password of a Marksman?

J.W.: I have.

S.W.: Will you give it to me?

J.W.: T...

S.W.: T...

J.W.: T...

S.W.: O...

J.W.: T...

S.W.: C...

J. W.: O...

S. W.: I... Have you a number?

J.W.: I have.

S.W.: What do you take for your number?

J. W.: Thirty-six.

S.W.: Why thirty-six?

J. W.: Because three times twelve are thirty-six.

S.W.: And what does that represent?

J.W.: The T... S..., the T... P... and the T... T... of the C... of I...

APPENDIX 5

Lecture Fifth Degree Blue

S.W.: Why do you wear that Robe?

J.W.: What Robe?

S.W.: That Blue Robe?

J.W.: As a sign or token of the Blue Order.

S.W.: Where are you from?

J.W.: The east.

S.W.: And whither are you going?

J.W.: To the west.

S.W.: Did you see anything as you travelled?

J.W.: The star that guided the wise men from the east and stood over where the young Child lay.

S.W.: Have you the entrance password of the Blue Degree?

J.W.: I have.

S.W.: Will you give it to me?
J.W.: I will if you begin.

S.W.: T...

J.W.: C...

S.W.: J... Why do you, as a member of the Blue Order, take T... C ... J... for your entrance password?

J.W.: Because he was the root and offspring of David, and the bright and morning Star.

S.W.: Did David see more than any other man?

J.W.: And David lifted up his eyes, and saw the angel of the Lord stand between the earth and the heaven, having a drawn sword in his hand and stretched out over Jerusalem.

S.W.: Have you a number?

J.W.: I have.

S.W.: What is your number?

J.W.: Four.

S.W.: What four?

J.W.: The four evangelists.

S.W.: Name them.

J.W.: Matthew, Mark, Luke and John.

S.W.: Did they receive any commission?

J.W.: They did.

S.W.: What was it ?

J.W.: Go ye into all the world, and preach the gospel to every creature, baptizing them in the name of the Father, Son and Holy Ghost, beginning at Jerusalem.

S.W.: Have you the sacred word of the Blue Degree?

J.W.: I have.

S.W.: Will you give it to me?

J.W.: No; but, finding you to be a true and worthy brother, I will letter it; so you begin.

S.W.: G...

J. W.: N...

S.W.: C... Why do you take G... for the sacred word?

J.W.: Because G... was the Word that was lost, and G... was the Word that was found.

S.W.: Where was it lost and found?

J.W.: It was lost at the building, and repairing of King Solomon's temple.

S.W.: How was it found?

J.W.: There occurred an upheaval of the earth which rent the temple in twain, and one of the men employed in repairing the rent found a scroll on which was written 'In the beginning was the Word, and the Word was with God, and the Word was God. The same was in the beginning with God. All things were made by Him, and without Him was not anything made that was made.'

S.W.: Have you the central password?

J.W.: I have.

S.W.: Give it to me. J.W.: H...

S.W.: U...

J.W.: T...

S.W.: L...

APPENDIX 6

Lecture Sixth Degree Blueman Master Builder

S.W: Brother, what are you?

J.W.: A Blueman.

S.W: A Blueman what?

J.W: A Blueman Master Builder.

S.W.: Where did Blueman Master Builders first assemble?

J.W: They assembled in the east and journeyed to the west.

S.W: Did they bring anything with?

J.W: They did.

S.W: What?

J.W: Signs, symbols and ceremonies.

S.W: Where did they obtain them ?

J.W: At the building of King Solomon's Temple.

S.W: How do you know that you are a Blueman Master Builder?

J.W: I am always taken and accepted as such by all Companions of that Degree.

S.W: How were you prepared for that honourable distinction?

J.W: I was divested of my outer garments, invested with a pair of blue overalls, held in position by a belt around my waist, and presented with a trowel, which was carried in my waist-belt.

S.W: Were you then admitted?

J.W: After being vouched for by the Senior Warden, who acted as my sponsor, I was.

S.W: How were you then dealt with?

J.W: I was led eleven times around the room, and then conducted to the Generalisimmo, who inquired whence I came, whither I was going, and for what?

S.W: What was your reply?

J.W: From the west to the east, to learn the mysteries of a Blueman Master Builder.

S.W: How were you then dealt with?

J.W: I was conducted twice around the room in a stooping posture, and presented before the three Grand Masters, who sat in the west: Solomon, King of Israel; Hiram, King of Tyre and Hiram Abif (the widow's son); to whom I made obeisance.

S.W: What was your next experience?

J.W: The Senior Warden having presented me, I was examined by the three Grand Masters as to my qualifications for participating in the labours necessary for the erecting of the temple.

S.W: What followed?

J.W: King Solomon placed a mallet in my right hand; Hiram, King of Tyre, a square in my left and Hiram Abif suspended a pair of compasses from my neck, after which he gave me the sublime keyword (or central password) of a Blueman Master Builder, and then ordered me to prove myself worthy of my work true and trusty.

S.W: What did you do with the sublime password?

J.W: I gave it to all my fellow workmen severally.

S.W: How were you next dealt with?

J.W: I was conducted to the preparation room, where the Senior Warden instructed me in the number of this degree and the proper knocks, after which I sought admission to the council chamber.

S.W: How did you gain admission?

J.W: By two knocks and a number.

S.W: How were they imparted ?

J.W: By mallet and mouth.

S.W: How were you further dealt with?

J.W: I was led twice around the room and again taken before the three Grand Master Builders, to whom I made obeisance. King Solomon then sent me to Hiram, King of Tyre, for examination, and he found me qualified to assume the obligation of a Blueman Master Builder.

S.W: How did you dispose of your working tools?

J.W: I placed the compasses on the north, the trowel on the south, the mallet on the west, while I stood in the east facing the three Grand Masters in the west, and, with the Bible in my right hand and the square in my left, took the solemn obligation of a Blueman Master Builder.

S.W: What is the number of this degree?

J.W: Eleven.

S.W: Why do you take eleven for your number?

J.W: Because it was in the eleventh year of the reign of King Solomon that the temple was dedicated and consecrated.

S.W: Give me the entrance password of a Blueman Master Builder?

S.W: K...

J.W: S...

S.W: Advance the hailing sign.

J.W. advances the hailing sign.

S.W: What does it denote?

J.W: The C... and S...

S.W: Why do you use this symbol?

J.W: Because King Solomon used the impression thereof on all official documents

S.W: Have you the grip of a Blueman Master Builder?

J.W: Hold your T...

S.W: Hold your T... Hold did you stand when brought to light?

J.W: Mid flames and thunder.

S.W: Have you the great and mighty grand password of a Blueman Master Builder?

J.W: I have.

S.W: Will you give it to me ?

J.W: I will if you begin.

S.W: U...and T...

J.W: T...and U...

S.W: T... p...

J.W: O...G...

S.W: B...G...

J.W: E...

S.W and J.W.: Amen.

APPENDIX 7

Lecture Seventh Degree White

S.W.: Why do you wear that Robe?

J.W.: What Robe?

S.W.: That white Robe.

J.W.: Because I am innocent.

S.W.: You are WHAT?

J.W.: I am even yet a stripling.

S.W.: Whence came you?

J.W.: From the sheepfold.

S.W.: Whither are you going?

J.W.: To the camp of Israel.

S.W.: What are you carrying there?

J.W.: Food for my brethren.

S.W.: What does it consist of?

J.W.: Loaves and cheeses.

S.W.: How many?

J.W.: Ten loaves and ten cheeses.

S.W.: How do you expect to get there?

J.W.: By the benefit of a password.

S.W.: Have you that password?

J.W.: I have.

S.W.: Will you give it to me?

J.W.: I will if you begin.

S.W.: G...

J.W.: A...

S.W.: T...

J.W.: L...

S.W.: B...

J.W.: W...

S.W.: T... Did you see anything there?

J.W.: A great sight.

S.W.: What was that sight?

J.W.: A man six cubits and a span, who defied the armies of Israel.

S.W.: Have you a number?

J.W.: I have.

S.W.: What do you take as your number?

J.W.: Five.

S.W.: What five?

J.W.: In token or representation of the five smooth stones I took out of the brook Kedron.

S.W.: How did you dispose of them?

J.W.: I placed them in a scrip or shepherd's bag.

S.W.: How did you further act?

J.W.: I put my hand in my bag, took thence a stone and slang it, and it sunk into the forehead of the Philistine, and he fell upon his face to the earth.

S.W.: How did you still further act?

J.W.: I advanced boldly, put my foot upon his neck, drew his sword out of its sheath, cut off his head, and bore it to the camp in triumph.

S.W.: Have you the central password of a White Companion?

J.W.: I have.

S.W.: Will you give it to me?

J.W.: I will if you begin.

S.W.: T...

J.W.: L...

S.W.: O...

J.W.: H...

S.W.: T...

J.W.: G...

S.W.: O...

J.W.: T...

S.W.: A...

J.W.: O...

S.W.: I...

APPENDIX 8

Lecture Eighth Degree Apron Green

S.W.: Why do you wear that apron?

J.W.: Because I am naked.

S.W.: Why are you naked?

J.W.: Because of my disobedience of the Lord's commands.

S.W.: Where are you from?

J.W.: The Garden of Eden.

S.W.: Whither are you going?

J.W.: To till the ground whence I was taken.

S.W.: How do you expect to get there?

J.W.: By the benefit of a password.

S.W.: Have you that password?

J.W.: I have.

S.W.: Will you give it to me?

J. W.: I will if you begin.

S.W.: T...

J.W.: F...

S.W.: S... What F... S...

J.W.: The sword that was placed eastward of the Garden of Eden, and which turned every way, to prevent Adam from eating of the tree of life and living forever.

S.W.: Have you a number?

J.W.: I have.

S.W.: What is your number?

J.W.: Six before and twelve behind.

S.W.: Your six before?

J.W.: In representation of the six days in which God created the heavens and the earth, and He also made man.

S.W.: Your twelve behind?

J.W.: In representation of the tree that grew in the midst of the garden, that bore twelve manner of fruits, and yielded its fruit every month, and whose leaves were for the healing of the nations.

S.W.: Have you the central password of an Apron Green man?

J.W: I have.

S.W.: Will you give it to me?

J.W.: I will if you begin.

S.W.: T...

J.W.: C...

S.W.: M...

J.W.: M...

S.W.: What C...?

J.W.: The C... that God gave to Adam, saying: 'Of all the trees in the garden thou mayest freely eat; but of the tree of the knowledge of good and evil thou shalt not ear, for in the day thou eatest thereof thou shalt surely die.'

APPENDIX 9

Lecture Ninth Degree Knight of the Green

S.W.: Why do you wear that ribbon?

J.W.: What ribbon?

S.W.: That green ribbon.

J.W.: As an emblem of the Knights of the Green.

S.W.: By this I perceive you are a Knight of the Green.

J.W.: I am always taken and accepted as such by all regularly initiated Knights of the Green.

S.W.: Where are you from?

J.W.: The plains.

S.W.: What plains?

J.W.: The plains eastward of Eden.

S.W.: And where are you going?

J.W.: To Mount Ararat.

S.W.: How do you expect to get there?

J.W.: By the benefit of a password.

S.W.: Have you that password?

J.W.: I have.

S.W.: Will you give it to me?

J.W.: I will if you begin.

S.W.: L...

J.W.: A...

S.W.: B...

J.W.: Y...

S.W.: S...

J.W.: C...

S.W.: T...

J.W.: W...

S.W.: A...

J.W.: A...

S.W.: F...

J.W.: O...

S.W.: T...

J.W.: E...

S.W.: Have you a number?

J.W.: I have.

S.W.: What is your number?

J.W.: One.

S.W.: Why do you take one as your number?

J.W.: In representation of the one window in the Ark.

S.W.: Have you another number?

J.W.: I have.

S.W.: What is it?

J.W.: Three.

S.W.: What three?

J.W.: The three sons of Noah.

S.W.: Name them.

J.W.: Shem, Ham and Japheth.

S.W.: What did you do at Ararat?

J.W.: Searched for the Mediterranean password.

S.W.: Did you find it?

J.W.: I did.

S.W.: Will you give it to me?

J.W.: I will; but you must first answer me a question or two.

S.W.: What are those questions?

J.W.: Where was the one window of the Ark placed?

S.W.: In the southeast corner.

J.W.: For what purpose?

S.W.: That Noah might see when the waters were assuaged from off the earth. Now that I have answered these questions, will you give me the Mediterranean password?

J.W.: I will if you begin.

S.W.: T...

J.W.: B...

S.W.: I...

J.W.: T...

S.W.: C... Why do you as a Knight of the Green take T... B... I... T... C... as your Mediterranean password?

J.W.: Because it contains all the colours I am entitled to wear; moreover it contains green.

S.W.: Of what was it a token?

J.W.: The covenant.

S.W.: What covenant?

J.W.: The covenant that God made with Noah, saying, 'I will no more destroy the earth with water for man's sake; in token thereof, I do set my bow in the cloud.'

S.W.: Give me the central password.

J.W.: T...

S.W.: C...

J.W.: E...

S.W.: N...

APPENDIX 10

Lecture Tenth Degree Gold

S.W.: Why do you wear that Crown?

J.W.: What Crown?

S.W.: That Golden Crown.

J.W.: As a token of the Gold Order.

S.W.: From this I perceive you are a Companion of the Gold Degree?

J.W.: I am taken and accepted as such by all Gold men.

S.W.: What colour do you choose?

J.W.: Gold.

S.W.: Why do you take gold for your colour?

J.W.: Because as gold is the purest of all metals when freed from dross, so should gold men be pure when tried in the furnace of affliction.

S.W.: Where are you from?

J.W.: The plains.

S.W.: And whither are you going?

J.W.: To Mount Gilead.

S.W.: How do you expect to get there?

J.W.: By the benefit of a password.

S.W.: Have you that password?

J.W.: I have.

S.W.: Will you give it to me?

J.W.: I Will if you begin.

S.W.: E...

J.W.: D...

S.W.: Why do you take E... for your password?

J.W.: Because it is the name of the pillar that was raised on the banks of the Jordan to distinguish the nine tribes and a half from the two tribes and a half: the tribe of Reuben, the tribe of Gad, and the half tribe of Manasseh.

S.W.: Have you a number?

J.W.: I have.

S.W.: What is your number?

J.W.: Ten.

S.W.: What ten?

J.W.: The ten Princes who wore ten crowns of beaten gold. Moreover, they wore robes of black edged with white.

S.W.: Have you the central password of a Gold man?

J.W.: P...

S.W.: V... Why do you as a Gold man take P... as your central password?

J.W.: Because it was from P... that King Solomon obtained the gold to make the vessels for the Lord's house, which shows that the gold from P... was the purest of all gold.

APPENDIX 11

Lecture Eleventh Degree Priestly Pass

S.W.: Brother, what are you?

J.W.: A member of the Priesthood.

S.W.: What proof have you to offer that you are?

J.W.: I have the Priestly Pass.

S.W.: Will you give it to me?

J.W.: I will if you begin.

S.W.: E...

J.W.: L...

S.W.: E...

J.W.: A...

S.W.: Z...

J. W.: A...

S.W.: R... Why do you take E... for your password?

J.W.: Because he succeeded Aaron as High Priest.

S.W.: How were you prepared for that degree?

J.W.: I was divested of all my outer raiment, invested with a plain white robe, also one adorned with bells and pomegranates. I was then elevated, and to sweet music and tinkling bells I was admitted into the sacred circle of the priesthood.

S.W.: Have you the central password of this degree?

J.W.: I have.

S.W.: Will you give it to me?

J.W.: I will if you begin.

S.W.: H...

J.W.: T...

S.W.: T...

J.W.: L...

S.W.: Why do you take H... T... T... L... for your central password?

J.W.: Because it was engraven upon the mitre on Aaron's forehead, that he might bear the iniquity of the holy things, and that they might be accepted before the Lord.

S.W.: Have you a number?

J.W.: I have.

S.W.: What is your number?

J.W.: Six.

S.W.: What does that represent?

J.W.: It represents the six holy garments worn by Aaron, the High Priest; viz., the breastplate, ephod, robe, embroidered coat, mitre and girdle.

S.W.: How were you received in this degree?

J.W.: I was properly clothed with the garments worn by the High Priest, and by him anointed as a priest for ever unto God and His righteousness.

S.W.: What are the two grand Christian virtues?

J.W.: Love of God and love of neighbour, which stand at the entrance of the Christian temple of the soul, and which are indispensable to the symmetrical completion of the Christian character.

ACKNOWLEDGEMENTS

There are a number of people whom I wish to acknowledge for their assistance in the writing of this book. I am grateful for the encouragement of Professor Oliver Leaman, University of Kentucky; The guidance offered by Prof Michael Lynch, University of Edinburgh: Prof Sean Connolly, Queens University, Belfast; Prof Alan Sharp, the University of Ulster; Dr M O'Dowd, Queens University, Belfast; Dr A D Buckley, Ulster Folk and Transport Museum; Dr Elaine McFarland, Glasgow Caledonian University; Dr A F Blackstock, Queens University, Belfast; D. Petri Mirala, Renvall Institute, University of Helsinki.

Ms Pamela Willis, curator of the Order of St John; The Very Rev Duncan Shaw; The Rev Hillis Fleming; Lesley Gent, *Bolton Evening News*; Pamela Godman, Local Studies Officer, Rochdale Council.

Mr C Kilpatrick, Archivist, Grand Orange Lodge of Ireland; David Cargo, Historian, the Loyal Orange Order and Royal Black Institution; Mr M E Phelan, Grand Secretary of the Grand Lodge of England; Tom Ferguson, Illustrious Order of Knights of Malta; David Bryce, Historian, Royal Black Institution, Scotland; Leslie J Loomis, Grand Commander, Knight Templar, Pennsylvania USA; the late Brother Sir Knight and Companion William Morrow, whose initial guidance and encouragement were invaluable.

Finally, my greatest debt is to my wife, Gillian (Cassy) for her support and encouragement.

BIBLIOGRAPHY

Annual Reports of the Imperial Grand Black Encampment, 1886-1933.

Atkenson, Donald Harman, Suprassing Wonder. The Inventions of the Bible and the Talmuds, Harcourt Brace and Company, Canada. 1998.

Attard, Joseph, The Knights of Malta, P.E.G. Publications, Malta.1992.

Bardon, J.A History of Ulster, The Blackstaff Press. Belfast. 1992, 2001, 200

Blackler, William and Wallace, Robert Hugh. The Formation of the Orange Order, 1795-1798. (edited papers) Grand Orange Lodge of Ireland publications. Belfast, 1994, 1999.

Bryce, David, A History of the Royal Black. Cadzow Publications Glasgow. 2001.

Bryce, David, The Triumph of the Imperial Grand Black Chapter. Cadzow Publications Glasgow. 2007.

Buckley, Anthony D and Anderson, T. Kenneth, Brotherhoods in Ireland, Ulster Folk and Transport Museum, Cultra, 1988.

Cargo, David, Brotherhoods in Newtownards in the 20th Century, Ards Historical Society. 2002.

Charles, James, A Report of the Annual Assembly of the Knights of Malta ex in Ireland. Dublin. 1850.

Clarke, J.R. The Change from Christianity to Deism in Freemasonry. Ars Quatuor Coronatorum.78. 1965.

Columbus York Rite –
www.columbusyorkrite.com. (U.S.A) website.

Cooper, Robert. L.D. Cracking the Freemasons Code. The Truth about Solomons Key and the Brotherhood. Rider. London. 2006.

Cordery, Simon British Friendly Societies, 1750-1914, Palgrave 2003. Houndmills and New York.

Cowan, Ian B, MacKay, P.H.R and Macquarrie, Alan, Knights of St. John of Jerusalem. Constable. Edinburgh. 1983.

Dawson, Kenneth L. Irish News May 20, 2003.

Dewar, James, The Unlocked Secret Freemasonry Examined. Corgi. London 1990.

Dewar, Rev.M.W,Brown, Rev.John and Long, Rev.S.E. Orangeism. a new historical appreciation. Grand Orange Lodge of Ireland. Belfast.1967.

Dickson, R.J., Ulster Emigration to Colonial America. 1718-1775. Routledge. London.1966.

Duby,Georges, The Chivalrous Society, trans Cynthia Postan, Edward Arnold, London.1977.

Ellert, Gerhart, Knights of St.John, trans J. Bockett-Pugh, Lutterworth Press. London.1958.

Eusebuis, Life of Constantine, trans Avril Cameron and Stuart G Hall. Oxford University Press. Oxford.1999.

Freemasonry Today, Winter 2000/2001. Issue 15.

Gilmour, T.H. Ancient and Modern: Imperial Grand Black Encampment of the Universe and Grand Black Lodge of Scotland. Kennedy, Robertson and Co. Glasgow. 1903.

Goldhill, Simon, The Temple of Jerusalem, Profile Books, London. 2004.

Gorsky, Martin, The Growth and distribution of English friendly societies in the early nineteenth century, Economic History Review.Vol 3 1998 p 503.

Gould, R.F. History of Freemasonry, Vol 1V. Caxton. London. 1936.

Grant, Michael. The Emperor Constantine. Weidenfeld and Nicolson. London.1993.

Healey, Edna, Part of a Pattern, Memoirs of a wife at Westminister, Headline Review. London. 2006.

House of Commons Select Committee Enquiry into the Orange Order, 1835.

House of Lords Select Committee on the State of Ireland, 1825.J. Murry. London. 1825.

Hutchens, Rex. R, A Bridge to Light. Supreme Council of the Ancient and Accepted Scottish Rite, Southern Jurisdiction. U.S.A. Washington. D.C. 1995.

Jackson, K.B., Beyond the Craft, Lewis Masonic, Addlestone. 1994.

Johnson-Link, E.M, The Development of the Ulster –Scottish Connection in Cultural Traditions in Northern Ireland. Ed John

Erskine and Gordon Lucy, The Institute of Irish Studies, The Queens University of Belfast. 1997.

Jones, Bernard E. Freemasons Book of the Royal Arch. Harrop. London. 1957.

Jones, Bernard. E, Freemasons Guide and Compendum. Harrop. London. 1988.

Kilpatrick, C.S, Murdie, Wm and Cargo, David, History of the Royal Arch Purple Order, Research Group.1993

Knight, Christopher and Lomas, Robert, The Hiram Key, Pharaohs, Freemasons and the Discovery of the Secret Scrolls of Jesus. Arrow. London. 1997.

Knoop, D, and Jones, G.P, The Genesis of Freemasonry. An Account of the Rise and Development of Freemasonry in its Operative, Accepted and Early Speculative Phases. Manchester University Press. 1947. 1978 published by Q.C. Correspondence Circle Ltd in association with Quatuor Coronati Lodge No 20`76. London 1978.

Gilbert. JT. History of Dublin, 1861. cited in History of the Royal Arch Purple Order. p10-11. Kilpatrick et.al.

Leaman, Oliver, Jewish Thought: An Introduction, Routledge. London. 2006.

MacLennon, W. J, Torpichen and the Knights Hospitaller. The Journal of the Royal College of Physicians of Edinburgh.33 (Suppl 12) 64-71. 2003.

Malta Bulletin. Grand Commandery of Pennsylvania Ancient and Illustrious Order Knights of Malta.1970-1973.

Manchester. The Oldest Royal Black Preceptory in Great Britain, Belfast Weekly News. 7 May, 1908.

Marrs, Jim. Rule of Secrecy. The Hidden History that connects the Trilateral Commission, the Freemasons and the Great Pyramids. Perennial. New York. 2001.

Marshall, William S, The Billy Boys: A Concise History of Orangesim in Scotland. Mercat Press. Edinburgh. 1996.

McClelland, Aiken, The Origins of the Imperial Grand Black Chapter of the British Commonwealth. Journal of the Royal Society of Antiquaries of Ireland, Vol 98. Part 2. 1. Dublin.

McClelland, A. Some Aspects of Freemasonry in the late 18th and early 19th century. Transactions of the Lodge of Research. 1958-1962. cited in History of Freemasonry in Meath. Larry Conclon.

McClelland, Aiken, William Johnston of Ballykilbeg, Ulster Society, Publications Ltd. Lurgan Co. Armagh. 1990.

McCrie T. Life of John Knox. Edinburgh. William Blackwood and Sons.1850.

Moore, W.A. The Irish Royal Arch Legend. The Research Chapter of New Zealand of Royal Arch Masons. No 95. Vol.6 No 2. (March) 1987.

Order of the Temple, The Grand Priory of Scotland. www.grandprioryofScotland.com. website.

Peakes Commentary on the Bible, eds Black, Matthew and Rowley, H.H. Thomas Nelson. London. 1962.

Penny, James, The Royal Arch Chapter and its place in the Development of Irish Freemasonry. Irish Lodge of Research. Dublin. 1923.

Piatigorsky, Alexander, Freemasonry.
The Study of a Phenomenon. The Harvill Press, London. 1997.

Porter, J.R. The Forgotten Bible. The Unknown Jesus, Visions of the Apocalypse. Prophets and Patriarchs.Watkins. London. 2007.

Radice, Giles.Friends & Rivals. Croslans, Jenkins and Healey. Abacus, London. 2003.

Rembower, T and Gray, Sir Frank, Ancient and Illustrious Order of Knights of Malta, 1948-1915. Supreme Grand Commandery Philadelphia, Pa. U.S.A. 1915.

Ridley, Jasper, The Freemasons, Robinson, London. 2000.

Rivals in Their Order, The New York Times, 6 January, 1890. (No author in the report).

Robbins, A, Secrets of the Tomb: Skull and Cross Bones, the Ivy League and the Hidden Paths of Power, Little ,Brown and Company. New York. 2003.

Rogers, Edward, History of the Royal Black Institution, 1857. (Unable to find place of publication and publisher).

Rules and Regulations of the Royal Arch Purple Order and Black Association. Protestant Journal Office. Belfast. 1846.

Sainty, Guy Stair, The Orders of Saint John. The History, Structure, Membership and Modern Role of the Five Hospitaller Orders of

Saint John of Jerusalem, the American Society of the Most
Venerable Order of Saint John of Jerusalem. New York 1991.

Sibbett, R.M. Orangeism in Ireland. 2 Vols.
Thynne and Co. Belfast.1939.

Sire, H.J.A. The Knights of Malta, Yale University Press.
New Haven CT. 1994, 1996.

Stevenson, D. The Origins of Freemasonry. Scotlands Century,
1590-1710. Cambridge University Press.1990.

The Holy Bible, Revised Standard Edition.
Collins. Great Britain. 1952.

The Royal Black Institution, Rochdale, Grand Chapter of the
Knights Templar. Belfast Weekly News. 24 May. 1906.

The Truth about Black Knighthood. Supreme Grand Encampment
of Ireland. Ballycastle. (Unable to find date of publication).

Vallance, Edward, Revolutionary England and the National
Covenant, State Oaths, Protestantism and the Political Nation,
1553-1682, The Boydell Press, Woodbridge, 2005.

Vermes, Geza. The Changing Faces of Jesus. London.
Penguin. 2001.

Wadron, Lamar and Hartmann, Thom, Ultimate Sacrifices: John
and Robert Kennedy, the plan for a coup in Cuba and the murder of
JFK. Carroll and Graf. New York. 2005.

INDEX

Lightning Source UK Ltd.
Milton Keynes UK
UKOW040328230313

208063UK00001B/23/P